Steps I̶ ̶ ̶ ̶ ̶ City

God at work in the life
of the founder of Birmingham
City Mission

EDWIN R ORTON

BIRMINGHAM CITY MISSION

First published 2006

Published by Birmingham City Mission
75 Watery Lane Middleway,
Birmingham B9 4HN

ISBN 13   978 0 9518307 1 0
ISBN 10   0 9518307 1 6

Biblical quotations are from the New International Version
© 1973, 1978, 1984 by the International Bible Society;
and from the Authorised Version, Crown copyright.

Book design and production for the publisher by
Bookprint Creative Services, P.O. Box 827, BN21 3YJ, England.
Printed in Great Britain.

Contents

Foreword by Peter Maiden
International Co-ordinator, Operation Mobilisation

As I write this Foreword I know that a few weeks from now, Edwin and his wife and co-worker, Dorothy, leave for India where they will be ministering to our OM Good Shepherd teams seeking to reach the poorest of the poor in India. These teams appreciate Edwin's ministry because they know it comes from a man who has lived what he teaches.

For sixty years God has led Edwin Orton to live a life which has glorified God and brought His blessing to tens of thousands in the United Kingdom and around the world.

You will be thrilled, as I have been, to read amazing incidents of God's guidance and of answered prayer in what seemed on occasion to be utterly impossible situations.

Enjoy this story for yourself then recommend it to your friends as it will inspire faith in all who read it.

January 2006

Introduction

Biographies of the rich and famous – and infamous – are much in demand today. It is not my purpose merely to add to that number. I am not one of those! Rather it is my intention to record acts of God in the life of an ordinary person in modern times.

In these days when success is measured by money or popular acclaim it is worthwhile to view life from another perspective, how God sees it. Faith is often perceived as a vague cliché, an uncertain emotion. Results of acts of faith are declared to be coincidences. Unbelief simply dismisses the facts as fiction. The word 'faith' is used as a synonym for philosophy, hence the term 'multi-faiths' but faith or trust alone can be quite dangerous. In whom we put our trust is more important than trust itself. Those who have been duped by confidence tricksters know this only too well. The sinking sands of wealth and popularity may look smooth and inviting but it is safer to stand on the Rock.

James, in the Bible, tackled this problem. He wrote,

> Show me your faith without deeds, and I will show you my faith by what I do. . . . Regarding Abraham he said that his faith and his actions were working together, and his faith was made complete by what he did . . . Faith without works is dead.

Apart from the fact that since the publication of my book *Into The City*[1] I have received many requests for more so I have become convinced that it is my duty to place on record the steps that led up to the forming of the Birmingham City Mission. Often I have been asked how I planned the founding of that organisation. The answer is simple; I did not plan it. All I did was follow one step at a time. The Lord went before and led the way. We may never know what greater things would have been achieved had we followed Him more nearly. This is the residue, the imperfect shadow of what might have been. But He knows our frame and remembers we are dust. His grace that is made perfect in weakness has been sufficient to bring us through.

That these events cover a period of over sixty years should add great weight to the author's conviction that they are not a series of flash-in-the pan episodes. Moreover, the lasting good that they have produced can be verified. Many of the people named are accessible today and will not only confirm the facts but will amplify the brief sketches that are written.

At the time many of the incidents seemed very matters of fact, nothing out of the ordinary. In isolation so they are. It is when they are considered as a whole that they testify to the faithfulness of a God who can be trusted.

The God who has led and provided through these years is the One who has been with his people across the centuries. He is still the same. Whole libraries of biographies and historical accounts of faith from around the world are available today. The Acts are still happening.

There is today a need among Christian workers to renew their simple faith. While we should not limit God in the means that He uses it is easy for us to be ensnared by the offers from government and fund-raisers. The advent of computer, e-mail, desktop publishing and other modern means of communication while useful are no substitute for prayer and faith. God has promised to supply our needs and so he will. Our wants are another matter. In those we need to carefully consider our motives. It does not hurt us to endure hardship or make sacrifices.

Let us remember that we are global Christians. We benefit from the prayers and faith of our brethren across the seas. They too look to us for spiritual and material support. In the past we sent out such men of faith as Hudson Taylor of the China Inland Mission, and a host of missionaries and reformers, men and women, who sowed the seed of the church that is blossoming today throughout the world. They set the pace. May we follow in their path.

Finally I wish to thank everyone who has had a part in this book. Many are mentioned by name but a host of others have prayed and given, have patiently helped in my discipleship and encouragement, not least of course, my wife Dorothy, our four children and their families. Special thanks are due to all the staff and members of Birmingham City Mission, and my secretary Pat Lambon. Thanks also to the members past and present of Kingshurst Evangelical Church whose love and encouragement mean so much.

At the end of an Income Tax Form is a statement that reads, 'To the best of my knowledge and belief . . .' All we have to do is sign it and it is legally binding. I willingly attach this statement to my version of *Steps into the City*.

How a Young Teenager
Found Faith

Men threw themselves from New York skyscrapers in the year that I was born. It was not my fault! 1929 was the year of the Wall Street crash heralding the Great Depression. The earth trembled and reeled in horror in the year of my New Birth, 1945. But that was not because of me either. The atomic bomb had exploded in Hiroshima.

News of the bomb and the end of the war with Japan awaited us when our group of Boy Scouts returned home from their summer camp near Worcester. At that time I was the leader of the troop. The closure of the troop in Marlborough Road School, Small Heath had been devastating to me because I enjoyed scouting so much. There had not been much for us to do during those war years. All the able-bodied men had been called up for military service and those who were left were busy doing war work. No one had time to take an interest in us boys. Most of our schoolteachers were women and the playing fields were used as anti-aircraft gun installations and barrage balloon bases.

The war had begun in September 1939 and most of the children in cities like Birmingham where I lived were evacuated to the country. A few like us had stayed behind.

Our education suffered because the local schools closed for about six months and when they did open it was for mornings only. We were in Redhill Junior School during the Battle of Britain and I well remember how we had sandbags at all the windows, the desks against the walls, and the regular air-raid drills when we dived under our desks. That autumn I moved up to the senior school. It was a disappointment to me as my teacher had entered me for the scholarship examinations for Yardley Grammar School. Not only did I pass but I was offered a free place at the prestigious King Edward School but we were poor and it was thought that we would not be able to afford uniform and books so the offer was declined.

Three weeks after I entered the Oldknow Road School it was bombed and we were without education again. When the school reopened it was co-educational, the gymnasium was closed, there was no science laboratory and recreation confined to the asphalt playground. However, after school I became a Boy Scout in Small Heath and had the joy of being taken camping in the Warwickshire countryside. Scouting therefore became a very important thing to me. Because I felt at such a loose end when the troop closed I had been glad to accept an invitation to a social evening at the nearby Friends' Institute where I had earlier attended a Sunday school run by Quakers. This led to me being asked to help in the Sunday school though I had little idea what it was about. Soon I asked if we could start a scout troop there. As we needed someone over twenty-one to be responsible a young man was persuaded to accept the post but he rarely attended. It was left to me to lead.

At that time I was requested to be the speaker at the evening service of the Friends' Institute. Why they asked me I do not know, neither did I know what to speak on or how to do it. Looking around for inspiration I opened the Sunday newspaper, *The People* and found a poem that attracted my attention. It was entitled, 'Why was I born?' With this before me I wrote out my first sermon (I was just sixteen). The time allocated was twenty minutes but when I finished delivering the talk I was embarrassed to find that it had taken only ten minutes. I therefore extemporised, waxing eloquent on the joys and value of scouting. In fact I began to wonder why I *was* born!

Camps were an integral part of scouting and therefore I felt it was my duty to arrange one. The first camp was at Easter 1945. With no adult to help and with all the wartime restrictions on travel and food rationing, not to mention that we had no money, we were rather limited. With a few shillings which I had earned we bought a second-hand tent. It needed proofing so following instructions in a magazine we made up a concoction, boiling it on my mother's gas stove, and applying it as it was suspended on the clothes line in the back garden. Somehow we got together some cooking utensils and the rest of our camping gear and set out for the Easter camp. We had little idea where we going but we boarded the nearest bus heading for the outskirts of the city. From the terminus we walked about a mile down a lane until we saw some inviting woodland. Finding a clearing we, that is about eight of us, pitched the tent and set up camp. It was a cold blustery spring but we enjoyed cooking on an open fire and being surrounded by the sights and sounds of natural woodland in stark contrast to the noisy dirty streets from which we came.

After the camping episode another important incident took place in my life. At the Sunday school teachers' meeting we were joined by a teenage girl whom I recognised as one who used to be in my class at school. She had a good singing voice and as juniors we had sung duets together. At the end of the Sunday afternoon sessions the teachers went for walks together and there the girl, Jean Tyler, told me about a book she was reading, *The Triumph of John and Betty Stam*[2]. As I was interested she gave me a copy.

For the first time I read of people who had a personal experience of God. They listened to Him, talked to Him and obeyed Him. What was more He answered them, guiding them through life and meeting their needs in amazing ways. They were a young American couple of Dutch ancestry, who had given up secure jobs and a comfortable lifestyle to become missionaries to China. I was so impressed by examples of their personal faith, as they trusted God to supply their needs as students at The Moody Bible Institute in Chicago. It was all so practical and real. One small incident stands out in my memory, when John Stam needed to make an urgent telephone call but he had no money. Eventually he went to the call box and was rewarded by finding that someone had left a coin beside the phone. The end of the story seemed very sad as they were attacked in their home in China by bandits who killed them leaving their baby in the ruins of their house.

Many years later I met a missionary couple in Norfolk who had known the Stams and entertained them in their home when first they arrived in China. Dorothy and I once visited Chicago and stood in awe in the great auditorium of The Moody Bible College during our visit. We heard how hundreds of young people offered themselves for missionary service at the memorial service following the martyrdom of John and Betty Stam.

The Triumph of John and Betty Stam had a dynamic effect upon me. At last I had a vision for my life. I wanted to be like them, which made me think that I had to become a missionary. It didn't occur to me that I needed to find God first. Naturally, I turned to the Sunday school superintendent Tom Goode for advice. He had known me for most of my life and he lived in the same road. I had been in his Sunday school class as a young child. He must have known that I came from a large family of six boys and one girl and that we were poor. My father was often out of work. This was common for men who had served in the First World War and went through the years of depression in the 20s and 30s. Tom had every right therefore to treat my enquiry about becoming a missionary as a bit of a joke. My main claim to fame was that I was usually up to mischief and involved in a fight. How could this sixteen years old boy who had left school two years earlier and was now training to be a plumber ever become a missionary to far-off lands? He kindly replied that I should give it more thought before he made enquiries on my behalf. To this I demanded to be told how long I should think and received the answer that I should wait six months. Surely I would have forgotten about it by then.

Several significant things were to happen to me during that time. One was that I found a leaflet on a table in my home. I don't know how it got there but I presume it had been given to one of my brothers or my father probably in a pub and he had emptied his pockets leaving this Christian tract on the table. It contained a series of verses from the Bible though I didn't know that. All that stood out to me were the words, 'But seek first the kingdom of God and his righteousness and all these things will be added unto you'. Matthew 6:33.

Who was this man Matthew who spoke with such authority? I soon discovered that they were actually the words of Jesus recorded in Matthew's Gospel in the Bible. After hunting around a bit in the house I discovered the Bible given to us as a prize some years before. It was the Authorised Version and in small print. Soon I was devouring my newfound treasure. This created a problem. I had always been an avid reader, at least ever since my teacher, Miss Penny, had inspired us with her wonderful stories and we had been taken to the newly opened public library in Yardley. But this was different; I was reading the Bible.

When you live in a small house full of people and with a radio blaring, you learn to cover your ears and concentrate if you wish to do some serious reading. Looking back I wonder how I read books by Charles Dickens, Rudyard Kipling and others not forgetting my beloved *Realms of Gold*, of the Children's Treasure House by Arthur Mee[3] which my teacher Miss Penny gave me.

The problem was The Holy Bible. Other books could be read in our house but this book was a challenge, an embarrassment, and a threat. It was made clear to me that I was not to read it, because it would drive me mad or cause some other trouble. I therefore started to go to bed early so that I could read in peace. When this was discovered I was ordered to put out the light. Not to be deterred I obtained a torch and read the Bible under the bedclothes. I was fascinated. Here was the world's greatest treasure, the Book of books. More than that it was the Word of Life to me, the answer that I had been seeking so long. It was no wonder that I soon bought a pocket New Testament to read on the bus and at work during the lunch break.

Tom Goode loaned me a modern version of the New Testament by Dr James Moffatt[4] and I was amazed to find that all the passages printed in verse were quotations from the Old Testament. This became a point of debate with Tom who doubted that the Bible could be trusted and raised the question of whether or not the Bible is the Word of God. At this time I did not know anyone who had the kind of faith of John and Betty Stam, and took God at His word, or talked to Him in a personal way.

A second significant thing that happened to me during this

time was a rather strange sudden experience. It was a beautiful summer Saturday morning and the sun was shining from a cloudless sky. We had to work on Saturdays until lunchtime. My job was to repair the guttering around a chimney on the roof of a terraced house. There were no problems and while I was working, my mind was on spiritual things. Everywhere that I could see from my advantage point was wonderful, the trees, flowers, birds and people. Surely there was some great plan for this entire great universe, and if by design there must be a designer. Did God exist? I could not doubt that He did. But did He care about His creation? Did He know or care about me?

The job was finished and it was time for me to pack up for the day. On the roof I had been working was a cat crawl ladder that lay across the slates. I had to lift this board onto my shoulder and carry it down the ladder from the roof to the ground, a distance of about twenty feet. Suddenly with a mighty crash I fell to the earth, the cat crawl and all. I missed the fence by inches, which could easily have broken my back. The commotion brought around all the neighbours, expecting to see me seriously injured. To my own amazement I stood rather shaken but without a cut or bruise. All I could think about was that He does know and care about me. He had answered my question Himself just as I was asking.

Now that summer was here it was time to take the lads to camp again. We had another camp in the spring when we had travelled by train to a small Warwickshire village and camped in a nearby field but it had rained all the time so we were glad to get back. Because the Scout Troop was growing, and in order for them to pass the tests I would need to teach them to swim, I decided I needed to learn to swim myself. As usual there was no man to teach us, so I went regularly to the local swimming baths on Sunday mornings and taught myself. This was important also because our next camp was to be beside the River Severn. One of my brothers told me about a suitable campsite a few miles from Worcester at Grimley on the riverbank. When the time came I loaded my bicycle with camping gear as no one we knew had a car. I then cycled from home to Worcester, about twenty-six miles then on another five or six to the campsite. There I pitched the tents and secured the gear and cycled back to Birmingham. Our small team of eight boys gathered and I put them on the bus to town, following them on my bike. We then all got on the train to Worcester taking the bicycle with us. Having put them on the bus to the campsite I followed again on the bike. It is surprising the amount of energy we have and what we can achieve when we are highly motivated.

The sequel to this story has an instructive twist. At the end of the week a man from the local farm came and took stock of the number of tents and campers and presented us with a bill saying he would call in the morning to collect the money. We had none. Furthermore we were astonished and enraged that we should be asked to pay at all. We were new to the ways of the world. Early next morning we were up, took down the tents and fled!

It was not until some years later when I was a Bible College student that my conscience caused me to write to the farmer and send him the money owing, plus interest.

Returning from the camp we learned that the war was finally over and that we had entered the nuclear age. But what had changed? On V.E. Day there had been dancing in the streets all night and people were relieved that the war was over. But for me there was sadness as so much suffering continued in the world. Also so many had profited from the war with high wages, black marketing and the plundering of the vanquished enemies. There was also the threat of atheistic communism whose propaganda was flooding the land. When we were in dire trouble the nation held a day of prayer but now there was no time for God. I was still seeking God myself but felt frustrated and in the dark.

By September six months had passed since I had expressed my interest in missionary work and been told to wait. It was on a Sunday evening towards the end of the month that a key event occurred. Still feeling rather lost and having no one to share things with I decided to go for a walk. I remember on leaving the house crying out, 'God, if you're there help me to find you.' It was often my practice to walk for a mile from my home towards Coventry. There is an area named after an inn that has long gone, called the Swan at Yardley. Turning right into Yardley Road I became aware of someone shouting. I crossed over to see what was going on and heard a man speaking to the passers by about God, the Bible, Jesus, heaven and hell. My first reaction was to hurry by, as I didn't want to get involved with some religious fanatics. But having walked a short distance I felt almost as if someone placed his hand upon my shoulder and told me to go back. I therefore returned and stood in a doorway down wind listening to the preacher. At once I knew that these people knew God as John and Betty Stam did. Here were those who took God at His word and experienced His reality. I was also challenged as they talked about sin and its consequences and the need to repent and ask for God's forgiveness. Much of this was new to me. Someone gave me a little booklet and I went away thoughtful but doing little else. Throughout the following week I continued to read my Bible and look up some of the passages mentioned in the book.

Somehow I couldn't wait until the next Sunday. At the same time in the evening I made my way to the Swan. How glad I was to see the meeting taking place again. This time I drew a little closer and at the end of the meeting asked questions about the message and also where they came from. They told me about the church in Waterloo Road and invited me to the evening service the following week.

Again I could hardly wait until the following Sunday. At the appointed time I made my way to Waterloo Road and went into the church. Looking around I was disappointed not to see any familiar faces, and that the choir and the minister wore robes. I also found it difficult to follow the service in the prayer book. However, if they had what I was looking for I would put up with all that. It was only when the minister preached his sermon that I knew that he didn't have what I wanted, a real knowledge of God. Sadly I left the church and nobody spoke to me. As I didn't know what else to do I went again to the Swan and was surprised to see the meeting again in progress.

'Where were you?' I asked, 'I went to your church and you were not there.' It soon became apparent that there were two churches in the same road and I had gone to the wrong one. God was teaching me the lesson that I would recognise His people by the life, which was in them, rather than by the clothes they wore or the building they attended.

A young man at the open air meeting, Stanley Marshall, took a special interest in me and seeing my disappointment at missing them at church invited me to a lecture being held the following week in Birmingham Town Hall. It was a lecture by an archaeologist on modern discoveries and the Bible. Only God knew that my greatest difficulty in committing my life to follow Christ was the question raised by the folks at the Quaker Sunday school and people in my own family, 'Is the Bible true?' That night when I listened to the archaeological professor talking about the findings at Ur of the Chaldees, Nineveh, Jerusalem and Jericho answered so many of my questions. Of course he didn't answer them all but I came to see that I was not being challenged by some idle tales but God was real and could be trusted. Above all I needed to put my personal faith in Him. However, considering the timeliness of this lecture, the only one of its kind I have ever been invited to attend, just when I was struggling over the authenticity of the Bible, the incident of the lecture itself was to me the work of God. I must say that I was astonished and encouraged to see about two thousand people seriously interested in the subject and most of them carrying Bibles.

On Sunday I attended the church with my new friends. It was called a Gospel Hall. I went there for some months before I learned that it was an assembly of the Open Christian Brethren. That was of no consequence to me, as I knew nothing about them. All I knew was that these people had a personal experience of God and that they were ordinary folks very much like the disciples of Jesus. They had a lot to teach me and I was eager to learn. Christian young people at the Gospel Hall, several of who were Sunday school teachers, invited me to have tea with them before the evening services. It was a good way of making friends. After tea I noticed some were going out. They said they were going fishing. I soon discovered they meant they were giving out Christian tracts and inviting people to the evening service. Going along with them I soon had a good conversation with a group of teenage boys who agreed to come with me to the meeting. Apparently no one had accepted the invitation before. When the boys were seated in the hall I went out to look for more and was again successful. After the service we all went into a small room at the rear where we had refreshments and talked about the Bible message.

Next week we repeated the process and again I was successful. This time, however we upset some church people by reserving seats for those we would bring in. As the service ended we heard the noise of more teenagers arriving so we quickly moved them to the back room. This time there was not enough space for us so one of the elders, Mr Aldridge, asked the remaining congregation to make room for us. He recognised that God was at work but there were those who didn't like their comfortable routine being disturbed. For several months following this 'Youth Hour' continued from about eight o'clock each Sunday evening.

The Christian young people were going on a ramble and they invited me to join them. As we walked through the Warwickshire countryside they told me they would arrive at a bank manager's house and hold a cottage meeting. Would I give my 'testimony'? This was a new word to me but I thought it meant give a small talk. I remembered the talk I had given at the Friends' Institute, but this was different. However, I agreed without knowing what it meant. We were soon crowded in the banker's lounge and given food. Then after a time of singing the leader announced that someone would give a testimony. To my relief it was a girl, Dorothy Perkins, whom I also remembered from school days. She just told of her own spiritual experiences, mentioning how her family had only recently become Christians too. Now I knew what I had to do. For the first time I told others of my own spiritual search and confessed that I had decided to be a follower of Jesus. I cannot describe the feelings of joy that now filled me. I did not know the Scripture that says, 'If you confess with your mouth "Jesus is Lord", and believe in your heart that God raised him from the dead, you will be saved.' (Romans 10:9) The distance between Dorridge where the meeting took place and my home was about eight miles which I walked that night with such joyfulness that I didn't notice the distance but felt I was walking on air.

My desire now was to learn as much as I could about the Christian life; I wanted to spend my life serving the Lord. When I learned that there was a service on Sunday mornings I wanted to attend though that meant a change in my lifestyle. We didn't normally get up until late so it required a real effort. The service was called 'the breaking of bread'. It consisted of an open time of worship without musical accompaniment and only the men being allowed to speak. This was new to me although I had attended one or two meetings of the Society of Friends, or Quakers, and they were similar but with no bread or wine. At the service I was treated like a visitor and not given the bread and wine. This I accepted but was surprised to notice that other young people I knew didn't take the bread either. Later I learned that they were refusing because I wasn't allowed to participate. The elders said that I could not partake until I was baptised. As I knew nothing of this practice I enquired about it and was shown that the Bible clearly taught that after one believed he should be baptised as a sign of repentance and union with Christ in his death and resurrection. When I saw it in the Bible I wanted to be baptised myself. But when my parents heard of my intention they were very upset and we had a great row. In retrospect now I would not advise other young people of sixteen to follow my example but I went ahead and got baptised and returned home with a bundle of wet clothing!

Learning to Serve

Live fish swim against the stream, but dead fish flow downstream. This is very true in the Christian life for there is certainly a current to counter. Opposition comes from every quarter, from within our own nature, and from without, including those who should know better. Those church members who had been disturbed by the arrival of numbers of lively young people unaccustomed to a religious culture raised their voices in opposition. Youths were rowdy, disrespectful, used unbecoming language and even smoked cigarettes in the church doorway! Soon the elders were compelled to announce the closure of the Youth Hour.

The young leaders of this project thought otherwise and acquired the use of a school right opposite my home. Each Sunday evening at eight crowds of teenagers packed the main hall hearing the Christian gospel presented in a way that they understood. The school had to be paid for but we had little money. We gave all we could and prayed for the rest. The money came and we were never in debt.

As the school building was so near my own house I invited my younger brothers to the meetings. I was already praying earnestly for them and one night I saw to my great delight that my brother Maurice was being counselled. Although he was only fourteen he decided to receive Christ and follow him. As we shared a bedroom it was wonderful to know that he shared the same spiritual interests.

My brother John who was between us in age was very opposed and sceptical but we were praying for him. As summer drew near I learned that there were to be some special evangelistic meetings held in a large tent in the city centre. Eventually we persuaded John to go with us. He had seen the change in our lives and in spite of outwardly appearing hostile he was interested. We were thrilled to see him go into the counselling tent and then hear that he too had decided to follow Jesus.

Again my interest in camping returned, but this time I wanted to put it to use in the Lord's service. So many young people were becoming interested in the Christian life but needed teaching. The idea was put forward that we should hold a camp at Easter. After making a number of enquiries we were able to secure the use of a small country school at historic Maxstoke, Warwickshire. Tents were put up in a nearby field for the boys while a classroom served as a Girls' Dormitory. Food was cooked in an improvised kitchen in the cycle sheds and the meetings were held in the assembly hall. The fun of being together in friendship and an eagerness to learn more of the Christian faith left a lasting impression on us all. It was so successful that we went ahead with a camp under canvas at another location in May.

In the summer of 1946 it was agreed that the young folks from the Gospel Hall should go on holiday together in Wales. An advertisement from a guesthouse in Barmouth was noticed so two of the young men went to see if the place was suitable. It was in a road with a long Welsh name and hard to find. They were riding their motor cycle near the promenade and saw an elderly couple walking along. Thinking that they were locals the boys stopped to ask them the way. Not only were they given the information they needed but they were asked if they knew the way to heaven. It transpired that they had asked the pastor of the local Congregational Church who was a keen evangelist and Bible teacher. Thus a friendship began with James and Grace Emblen. That holiday in Barmouth was unforgettable for me. For one thing I had never been on holiday before. My parents couldn't afford such a thing as it was in the days when working men only got Bank holidays off and then they were not paid for them. My mother used to dread a 'short week'.

More importantly this was a Christian holiday made special to me because of the Bible teaching of James Emblen. Each morning he climbed the steep hill from his small house beside the harbour up to our guesthouse and there opened to us the great truths of the Word of God. The Emblens had met when James, a widower, was holding tent missions in Cheshire. He was a preacher and children's evangelist of repute serving abroad in Australia, Canada and the United States of America. I once met a missionary working in Brazil who told me he was converted at a beach mission led by James Emblen. Apart from his teaching he and his wife were great people of prayer and faith. Extracts from his diary were like those of the great George Müller who trusted God to supply all his needs for the famous orphanage in Bristol.

We were delighted when their daughter Grace came to stay with them. She was on furlough from China where she served as a missionary with the China Inland Mission, the same society in which John and Betty Stam had worked. Communist bandits had captured Grace Emblen and force-marched over mountain trails until she miraculously escaped. Her story is told in *The Restraining Hand*, by Alfred Bosshardt[5]. Can you imagine my joy and wonder at being in such a company? It was even more so when other guests joined us at the house party and as there was no room for so many I was invited to stay at the Emblens' house.

The two Sundays we were there were particularly busy. The church on the promenade was full for the morning service, then there were open-air meetings, beach meetings, evening gospel services and finally back to their house for a wonderful time around the Lord's Table. A significant event for me at that time was that my friend John Harvey also had to move out of the guesthouse and share a room with me in the Emblens' home. We had some good conversations and I learned that he worked at the Queen Elizabeth Hospital in Birmingham as an operating theatre orderly. I shared with him my vision that one day I wanted to be a missionary. It was almost a year since I had found Christ. I had hardly missed a meeting at the Gospel Hall since then and was reading widely and studying the Bible earnestly. But what would be the next step. It was hard for a young man with limited education and no money or influential friends. John told me about his work and said that the hospital was about to start training men as nurses. This could be a useful thing to do as a step towards training for the mission field.

The holiday ended, leaving me with memories of a glorious summer resplendent with magnificent sunsets over the western sea and climbing my first mountain, Cader Idris. Then rowing down the beautiful estuary under the railway bridge over which steam engines of the Great Western Railway ran, and walking near Lake Bala and hearing the enchanting story of Mary Jones and her Bible that led to the founding of the British and Foreign Bible Society. Such holidays disappear into the past as a lovely interlude detached from real life. This was not to be for me. On my return to Birmingham I prayed earnestly for guidance about my future and felt that I should write to the Queen Elizabeth Hospital applying for a job that would pave the way for me to receive training that would be useful in overseas missionary work. To my amazement and joy I was offered an interview with the Matron. In spite of what was to me an awesome occasion I believed the interview went well and I was confident that I would get the position. John Harvey had some Christian friends who were due to get married at Boston in Lincolnshire. He invited me to join him, offering to transport me on the back of his motor cycle. For this I needed permission to be absent from work on a Saturday. As I mentioned earlier that was a workday and I was still employed by the builders for whom I fell off a roof!

At that time I was having other difficulties with my employers because I came to realise that they were involved in corruption and they were asking me to sign documents in order to make false claims. When they refused to give me the day off for the wedding I decided that this was the time for me to resign. After all, wasn't I soon to begin working at the hospital? But I was wrong.

A few days later I received a letter telling me that my application had been unsuccessful. I was devastated. The conviction that I was now at an important crisis in my life, that my motives were right and that God was calling me made me determined to try all possible doors. Maybe there were other hospitals that would open their doors to me and provide the opportunity I was looking for. I therefore began writing to all the hospitals I knew in the Birmingham area. One by one the answers came. No one was interested. The door seemed to be solidly closed. Of course I was also now unemployed, and as this was before unemployment money was available to people like me I was fast running out of funds.

In our household everyone was expected to work and contribute to the family income. My mother herself was I think the hardest working person I ever knew personally. She had no time for lazy layabouts. When the day came that all my small savings had gone and I had to tell her I couldn't give her my contribution towards the housekeeping she was very angry. I suppose my new lifestyle was already giving her problems and she was afraid that I was getting far too deep into religious things and now it was time for it to end. She shouted at me and told me to forget all this nonsense about being a missionary and that I should go out and get a job, any job and that she wouldn't keep me unless I earned some money. It seems that God has to bring us very low before He can really bless us. When we have no one else to turn to and we genuinely call upon the Lord He is pleased to reveal Himself to us. This was certainly so in this case.

We lived in a small three bedroomed terraced house in Francis Road, Hay Mills. As I write, the house still stands. In those days the living room was in the middle of the house while the front room was the best room reserved for visitors. It was to this front room that I retired in my misery having been strongly rebuked by my mother. I fell on my knees and wept before the Lord. I felt that somehow the rebuke was against Him and that I had let Him down. Had I done wrong to leave my job? Was God really calling me to serve Him? Would He not help me in this my time of need? While I was kneeling in prayer I heard footsteps come up to the front door and something was passed through the letterbox. I got up and went into the hallway to see what it was, not expecting it would be for me as apart from job applications I never corresponded with anyone else. Imagine my surprise on seeing a letter addressed to me. Also, why then? It was four o'clock in the afternoon, past time for the delivery of mail.

Quickly I tore open the envelope. To my amazement there was no letter, just a plain piece of paper and a ten shilling note. That was not a great deal of money then but of much more value than it would be today, and for me it was riches beyond description. The timing was perfect. My heavenly Father knew and cared as He has continued to throughout these more than sixty years since I committed my life to Him. With tears I returned to kneel with thankfulness beside the front room couch. Then I went through to the kitchen where my mother was still working when she had scolded me just a short while earlier. When I presented her with the ten shilling note she protested that I had told her that I had no money. I then showed her the envelope. It had a post mark indicating that it had been posted the day before. I had no idea who had sent it, neither do I know to this day. But I told her what had happened and that I had asked God for His help. She received the money reluctantly but gratefully for she needed it, but her anger went and she never raised the matter of money with me again.

A day or two later while reading the *Birmingham Evening Mail* I noticed an advertisement inviting applications from young men to train to be nurses at Oldchurch Hospital in Romford, Essex. This was just what I was looking for, though I had never heard of Romford before. Immediately I wrote off and applied. This time to my surprise and joy I was accepted. The only proviso was that I should obtain some reading glasses, a fountain pen and a watch, none of which I possessed at that time. Also the post was non-resident so I needed to find lodgings. I wrote to the hospital matron asking her help as I knew no one in Romford. She sent me the name and address of a local Baptist minister who kindly announced my need to his congregation that resulted in my need being met.

The day came for me to leave Birmingham and travel for the first time to London and on to Essex. The evening before my departure was the usual Bible study at the Gospel Hall. When Mr Aldridge, the leader heard that I was leaving he gathered people around and prayed for me. One of the young men said, 'I expect you are going to live with the Emblens.' 'Oh no,' I replied, 'they live in Barmouth in Wales.' 'Don't you know that their real home is in Romford, Essex?' he exclaimed. I could hardly believe it. The only advert I had ever seen for the course I wanted came from the very place where the friends who had been such a spiritual help to me lived. I had no idea that James Emblen had taken the post of pastor of the Barmouth Congregational Church as a temporary position during the summer holidays. On the evening of my arrival in Romford the Emblens had an unexpected visitor!

Learning to Suffer

Radical changes were taking place everywhere in post-war Britain of the forties. Occupied as we were with the advent of the welfare state under the new Labour government, we were hardly aware of the demise of the Indian Empire and the dreadful massacres following Partition, nor the new era about to begin with the formation of the state of Israel. In England we were more concerned with rebuilding and repairing war damaged property, and re-training the demobilised armed forces with skills to win the peace. Much work needed to be done. Homes were overcrowded, luxuries were few and food was still rationed. Those who worked in institutions like hospitals were even less aware of historic world events. But important new discoveries were making an impact on everyday lives. For instance the hospital ward to which I was first allocated was orthopaedic. Many patients suffered from the terrible osteomyelitis, a painful chronic illness that recurrently required long periods in hospital. There was an excitement about the place when a new treatment was introduced called penicillin. Within a few weeks patients who had spent years bedridden were up and about ready to be discharged.

It had been a radical change for the hospital to begin training men as nurses. We were the first group and of course all senior staff were women, many of who did not approve of male nurses. Hospital routine was rigid and strict protocol had to be observed. For me it was good training in humility. Everything was new, challenging and exciting. It was good to see people being healed, but I also saw others die and felt the pain of grief. There was the young sailor with bone cancer who became addicted to the heroin that was his only relief from excruciating pain. There were the ex-soldiers who still needed shrapnel removed from their bodies. Then there were the sick children whom we learned to love and care for as if they were our own.

My hospital training was rudely interrupted by the fact that I was approaching my eighteenth birthday and was required by law to register for national service. This caused me a great deal of heart searching. Before my conversion there was nothing I liked better than to have a fight. Regularly I had attended boxing lessons in Jenkins Street evening school Small Heath. I had even tried to join the army as an apprentice before my parents found out. Now things were different. My study of the Sermon on the Mount had given me another view on life. Besides how could I be a missionary and a messenger of God's love and yet be prepared to kill? It had already come to my notice that British law allowed objections to military service on grounds of conscience. I therefore decided to object, hoping at the same time that I could continue my hospital training. The day came when I joined the queue at the labour exchange to register. When it came to my turn I said, 'I want to register as a conscientious objector.' There was a gasp from the clerk. The queue froze and all eyes were upon me. It took some time for the officials to find the appropriate forms and discover the correct procedure, as they not had a case like this before. Soon I was back in my lodgings trying to fill in the answers and compose a statement to explain the grounds of my objections. This was made a matter of prayer and I resolved that I would not seek the help of anyone but God and that whatever the outcome I would accept it as His will.

In due course I was summoned to a tribunal in Fulham, London to be heard by the renowned Judge Hargreaves. It was an awesome experience to be cross-examined in a court where we were made to feel like criminals. The aim of the questions was to find out if our objections were really a matter of conscience or if we had some ulterior motive for avoiding military service. Solicitors or other professional advisors accompanied most objectors, but I had gone alone. When it was my turn I gave an account of my history thus far and how I had arrived at my conclusions by studying the Bible. After discussing my case with others on the bench the Judge announced that I must go into the army and serve in the Non Combatant Corps. This was a new thing to me, as I had never before heard of the NCC. As I left the court an official whispered to me, 'You can appeal, you know.'

The formal statement of the Tribunal arrived I was given the option, so as this was all part of the legal process I decided to appeal. A few weeks later I was summoned to appear before an Appellate Tribunal in Westminster. It was a daunting prospect to enter the grand buildings near to Westminster Hall and be questioned by three members of the House of Lords. I answered the same way I had done before telling of my conversion and desire to serve God with a good conscience. There was an adjournment and then they returned to ask me to come on another occasion but to either bring someone with me or get letters of support. This put me into a difficulty because I really wanted to be in the will of God and had decided to ask Him alone for help. However, to comply with the court's instructions I went to the hospital matron and explained the situation. She responded by writing a letter simply confirming my position in the hospital and vouching my good character.

The morning of my third tribunal was beautiful and sunny. I was confident that this time my application for exemption from military service would be successful. Again I was questioned by the three peers of the realm and it sounded as if they were really on my side. They seemed disappointed that I hadn't brought someone to argue my case. At the close of my final statement I declared my faith in God and that I believed He would guide them to the right decision and that I would accept whatever they said. As I look back I am amazed at my boldness and wonder if it was seen to be impertinent. However, they were very kind which made it even more of a blow when they returned to announce that my appeal had been rejected and that I should go into the Non-Combatant Corps.

The news stunned me. Why was this happening when God had so clearly led me to take up the course in hospital in Romford? What would be the purpose of going into the army when I needed to prepare for the Lord's service?

Feeling so bewildered and downcast I wandered out of the building and on to the street. Almost next door stood the ancient Westminster Abbey into which I had never entered before. Somehow I felt drawn inside and so shuffled in head downwards. Suddenly I was reading in letters of gold, 'And other sheep I have, which are not of this fold: them also I must bring, and they shall hear my voice; and there shall be one fold, and one shepherd.'

They are of course the words from the Bible (John 10:16) inscribed around the tomb of David Livingstone on the floor of the central aisle just inside the Abbey. God has spoken to me in many ways but this will always be precious to me. He knew the sincere motives of this young man and his disappointment and He gave reassurance and purpose. Immediately the gloom lifted to be replaced with excited anticipation of the future. The Lord had other sheep and He was in the business of bringing them back. His plans of other ways for me were in some way connected with this.

While working on a hospital ward in February 1947 I received a nasty shock. Mrs Le Fevre, a Christian peripatetic teacher who taught sick children came with the news that Mr Emblen had died of a heart attack. It must have been shortly after my last visit to his home. That winter was very severe with heavy snow. Mrs Emblen was in Barmouth, Grace had returned to China and James living alone had decided to clear the snow. He was a big man with a booming voice and a hearty laugh but the effort was too much for him and he collapsed. It was two or three days later that the news came to me but I realised that I was probably the last person to see him in good health (I had visited him one evening when he was alone.) Hurriedly I rushed to see his wife who had now returned from Wales. It was a fresh experience for me but I wanted to offer help. 'Ma' Emblen, as we used to call her, answered the door. 'Come in,' she said calmly, 'it must have been a nasty shock for you!' I never heard her complain. She was just concerned for others but she lived so near to the Lord that it seemed that He was there and nothing had changed. One of her hand painted scrolls was pointed out to me. It said in the Old English of the King James Bible, 'But Thou remainest'. The story of Ma Emblen would make an excellent topic for another book. No one else I ever knew had such a practical personal faith or had such a close walk with God. Without doubt she had a great influence upon my life and taught me a great deal. All sorts of projects in Essex, at Kingshurst, in the Birmingham City Mission and overseas would hardly have been achieved without her prayerful, financial backing.

Not least among the quiet guidance she gave me was an invitation to a Bible conference at Easter 1947. There I met missionaries and Christian leaders who were fully committed to following the Lord at whatever cost. Some were national workers from India, China and South America. The Bible teaching was given by T Austin-Sparks, a scholarly Scotsman with spiritual vision often misunderstood but whose ideas are now commonplace among evangelical Christians. Three meetings were held on Good Friday, two on Saturday, three on Sunday and three on bank holiday Monday. We attended them all and as it took an hour and a half for us to get there from Romford each day Ma Emblen provided me with food. This conference was the first of many which I attended over a number of years and which helped me to think deeply about many issues concerning the work of God in the world at this time. It is interesting to note that the conference centre at 39 Honor Oak Road, Forest Hill, London is now the base from which George Verwer co-ordinates the world-wide missionary activities of Operation Mobilisation.

Before I left my situation in Romford I received wonderful news from my home in Birmingham. At the end of six months on the training course I had been allowed to go home for a holiday. This lasted for two weeks during which to prevent any controversy I refrained from talking to those who were not believers about my faith. In the past my mother had been particularly hostile so it was not until the final day which was a Sunday that I told her that I had been invited to preach at the Gospel Hall and wondered if she would like to come to hear me. To my amazement she consented to accompany me. How excited I was and how hard I prayed for her. She was very quiet after the meeting, but I didn't press her about anything. The next morning I returned to Essex. About ten days later I received the joyful news that my mother had decided to follow the Lord and had received Him into her life. Soon after I heard again that she had been baptised as a believer. I was so sorry not to have been there and I am equally sad not to have retained those letters.

A few months later I was again invited to preach at the Gospel Hall. My sister's husband called on my mother and she invited him to hear me. Billy Murch was not interested. He had been a professional jockey and travelled around the world. Although as a stable lad at Newmarket he had attended a Bible Class he had long dismissed the idea of God from his mind. He even said to my mother that he was surprised that a woman of her age should believe such things. I knew nothing of this conversation but nevertheless was amazed to see Billy in the congregation. The Lord dealt with him and before he left the building he had broken down and received Christ as his Saviour. He became an earnest follower of the Lord, constantly sharing his faith in the car factory where he worked and serving Him faithfully for many years until he went to be with Christ. My sister Jessie also became a devout believer and at the time of writing she is in her eighties serving the Lord joyfully at that same Gospel Hall.

Led Into the Wilderness

The Midland Red bus from Birmingham to Stourport-on-Severn deposited me within walking distance of the huge bleak army camp which was to be my base for a while. Having no idea what to expect I was surprised that no others seemed to be arriving at the same time. Soon I was taken to the Quartermaster's office and kitted out with uniform and equipment, but of course no weapons. Then I was led to a crowded barrack room and allocated a bed. As I began to unpack my few belongings I remembered being warned that unless I took an early stand as a Christian it would be very difficult for my faith to survive. Seeing my Bible in my bag I therefore nervously placed it on my bed. To my astonishment a few moments later I noticed that on my neighbour's bed there was also a Bible! Derrick Waller was the only other man who had joined up that day and he was a Christian. We became firm friends and still keep in touch to this day.

The camp was a vast training centre for the Royal Pioneer Corps. They were the builders of roads and diggers of trenches, the labourers for whom the NCC men were drafted in to do most of their clerical and administrative work. At the end of the war the army declared an amnesty for deserters provided that they gave themselves up. Such people were also sent to this camp for dishonourable discharge because of their crimes, or medical discharge because of mental problems, an easy way out for everybody. All such soldiers were under arrest so there was both a kind of open prison and a tightly secure prison on the campus. Both these sites were the scenes of regular spectacular escapes.

Nearby was the Medical Inspection room to which I was immediately attached because of my past nursing experience. Each morning about a hundred of this motley crew of some of the roughest men in the army reported on sick parade. Our job was to treat their everyday injuries and sicknesses and also prepare reports for the psychiatrists, medical boards and court-martials. It became a bit dangerous at times but we had plenty of fun. It was also a good opportunity to witness for Christ. No one stopped us from putting out tracts on the chairs in the waiting room or following up with personal conversations. NCC was well known to a group of Christians known as the Exclusive Brethren and many of them were in the camp. Those who didn't belong to the sect were denied fellowship but the rest of the Christians of most denominations worked together.

We were sometimes called 'Non-Commissioned Chaplains'. There were early morning prayer meetings and lunchtime Bible studies when small numbers managed to eat at the same tables in the huge dining halls, which catered for thousands of soldiers. Permission was granted for us to enter the prison blocks to hold gospel services some evenings. On one occasion we were attacked and our musician had his piano accordion destroyed. But we learned many lessons and I realised that my training for the mission field was continuing. The climax of it all was when we were allowed to put on an evangelistic crusade for the whole camp. The camp theatre was put at our disposal and the chaplain helped by letting us use his jeep to which we attached a loud speaker and drove around announcing the meetings. A male voice choir was formed and the small group of evangelical Christians gave testimonies and preached. The meetings were well attended not only by young trainees from the lower camp but also by officers including the colonel Commander-in-Chief.

This time was a very formative period in our lives. Most of us were in our late 'teens or early twenties. We carried Bibles or New Testaments in our uniform breast pockets and often these scriptures were consulted during informal discussions on some theological point. Among those present was Geoffrey Grogan who influenced me to go to BTI Glasgow. Later he went on to be Principal of that Bible College and wrote extensively on theological matters.

Some of us were invited to homes of local believers. Mr and Mrs Young-Johns of Kidderminster put their home at our disposal. These godly folks made a great impression on us. Mr Young-Johns worked in a carpet factory where he was a keen witness for Christ. He frequently preached in the open air. One day I was invited to go with him and his friend Pearson Chamings to preach on a housing estate. Mr Chamings was impressed by my preaching and wrote to the elders of my church. I knew nothing of this until I was on leave and they told me. Such kind acts of encouragement can be an enormous help to a young person.

I heard Mr Chamings preach on many occasions. He held a responsible post as Director of Public Health for the county of Worcestershire. When founding the Birmingham City Mission it seemed natural to me to invite him on to our Council of Reference. He was also chairman or our Inaugural Meeting in October 1966.

At the end of 1947 the Royal Pioneer Corps training centre was moved to Blackmoor No 1 Camp near Great Malvern. In the setting of the undulating Worcestershire countryside in the shadow of the beautiful Malvern Hills thousands of young soldiers received their basic military training. The medical unit was busy dealing with injuries from the assault course and the usual emergencies associated with a large community. Medical inspections and prophylactic injections were given to those who were to serve overseas. So much valuable experience was gained which would later be used in my missionary work abroad.

In Great Malvern we found Christian fellowship at Cowleigh Road chapel attended by pupils and staff of the Clarendon Girls' School. Harold St John, former missionary and father of author Patricia St John, was the headmaster. Each Sunday morning we listened spellbound to his scholarly Bible expositions. Some members of the congregation were scientists employed on highly secret radar work at the nearby Technical Research Establishment.

Cowleigh Road Chapel was responsible for another small Gospel Hall on the common near the small village of Guarlford. Called 'The Old Elm' it consisted of a tiny collection of wooden huts. A few elderly ladies made up the congregation and Mrs Edwards, who acted as a kind of mother to many Christian young soldiers, played the old organ. They very much welcomed my presence and allowed me to practise my preaching. There were no children in the church and as, by this time, my friend Stanley Marshall was a Children's Evangelist in Birmingham. I invited him to come and look at the hall with a view to holding a mission in the village. The elders responsible in Malvern were against it so it never happened but the contact was important for eventually the hall was bought as a camp centre for children from Birmingham under Stan Marshall's leadership. It was a great blessing to many over a number of years until it developed into the Gaines Youth Centre at Whitbourne where it is now.

In response to my request the elders suggested that I might like to start a children's work in their own hall in Cowleigh Road, as they had no Sunday school. The population of North Malvern was larger than Guarlford so I felt challenged to do something. Looking back I wonder how we managed. The camp where I served as a young soldier of twenty years was more than three miles away, mostly uphill, from the chapel. The only other people offering to help were the elderly Mrs Edwards and her daughter Stella. We got some invitation cards printed and cycling out of the camp and up the hill on several evenings I managed to visit most of the homes in the district. It drew in forty boys and girls to attend the mission each evening for a week resulting in the start of a new Sunday school which I understand continued for many years.

Early in 1949 our unit was moved once more, this time to Seighton Camp Chester. The city was the hub of much military activity and I was drawn into the work of the Army Scripture Reader, Mr Samuel, father of the well-known Bible teacher Leith Samuel. He held evangelistic meetings in a YMCA in the camp. When he became ill it fell to me to take his place for a while arranging the meetings and doing some of the preaching.

The first Fact and Faith films, *God of Creation* and *Dust or Destiny* were released at that time and we showed them to the troops wandering about the city. The basement of the central Baptist church was filled with soldiers and airmen on Sunday evenings as they were given refreshments while the listened to the gospel.

The Samuels belonged to the local Brethren and I often attended their meetings and did some preaching in the open-air. Their home was open to us young Christian soldiers where they fed us physically and spiritually. Mrs Samuel was a saintly lady who taught us to appreciate the words of some of the great hymns. I can still hear her lovely Scottish voice reciting from Katherine Kelly's great hymn,

> Give me a sight, O Saviour . . .
> Was it the nails, O Saviour that bound Thee to the tree?
> Nay, 'twas Thine everlasting love,
> Thy love for me, for me.

One evening in their home I was surprised to find a table spread in my honour and that they had baked a cake for my twentieth birthday. I never found out how they knew it was my special day. What wonderful lessons in Christian hospitality we learned from those godly people.

In spite of all these activities in Chester I used to feel quite lonely at times. My friend Derrick Waller who joined the army on the same day as me was still with me. He told me about the girl whom he intended to marry. I then spoke to him about Dorothy Perkins, whom I had met at the open-air meeting that played such an important part in my conversion. We had known each other since early school days and now she was in her final year of nursing training with a view to becoming a missionary. A relationship had begun to form just before I joined the army. She had a day off duty and had nothing to do so I suggested that she and her brother Fred, who was later to become a missionary to Algeria, should join me in cycling to the village of Coleshill delivering Christian tracts. From then I had often visited their home and after enlisting had taken her to stay with Mrs Emblen for a weekend while attending a conference at Honor Oak. After that the friendship ended and we seldom saw each other.

I think it was Derrick's idea that as almost two years had elapsed since that time I ought to write to Dorothy and ask if I could meet her again. Obviously she agreed! Derrick and I travelled together to Aldershot to get demobilised. We had been together a great deal for exactly two years yet strangely we did not meet again until an NCC re-union forty years later when we renewed our friendship as if it were but yesterday.

Learning to Trust

Conscription into the armed forces is a disruption in anyone's life but not necessarily a waste. In my case I had learned a great deal and acquired valuable experience. Nevertheless on returning to civilian life I was unsure of the future. Where could I pick up the threads of missionary training? Firstly I was able to spend a wonderful couple of weeks at the Kilcreggan conference centre in Scotland which belonged to the Honor Oak Christian Fellowship. The building was later donated by them to the Worldwide Evangelisation Crusade (WEC), an act which I greatly admired.

On my return home I was confident that the Lord was going to open the way for me to continue my studies or provide me with a job. No way was I going to look for work in the usual way. I was sure it would come miraculously. However it didn't and my meagre funds were getting low.

Although this time my mother was not chiding me I did not want to become a burden to her so one morning I reluctantly went to the labour exchange.

As I sat waiting my turn to be interviewed I noticed a door with a sign saying, 'Rehabilitation Advice'. It was a strange notice and I had time to ponder on its meaning. Suddenly it occurred to me that it could be for me. The door opened into a busy office. There was a receptionist and I asked if they were able to help ex-servicemen. When he agreed I blurted out, 'Does the government provide grants for people like me to go to Bible College?' He looked nonplussed and having never heard of such a thing before, he got on the telephone for help. After a while to my embarrassment he called across the office, 'Is it anything to do with church work?' Soon he returned with a card to say that I had an appointment that afternoon with someone who may be able to advise me.

The Appointments Office in Broad Street was very upmarket from the Small Heath labour exchange. The interviewer answered my enquiry by immediately asking which Bible College I was interested in. This took me by surprise and at first I could only think of the London Bible College with which I was studying on a correspondence course. However I knew next to nothing about the college and knew no one who had been there. Then I remembered that Geoffrey Grogan, who was with us in the NCC at Stourport, had gone to the Bible Training Institute in Glasgow. If it were good enough for him it would be good enough for me. The lady produced a book and astounded me by saying that the Government approved the College. In astonishment I asked if it was at all possible that I could get a grant to go to Bible College. She replied that there was a scheme for those whose training had been interrupted and had entered the forces before September 1947. Of course I had evidence of my hospital training being interrupted and that I had joined the army in August 1947. These things may sound matter of fact to the reader but for me who had no idea of such possibilities, to see how things had been ordered to such fine detail was miraculous. The experience I had gained in the army and the studies at BTI were to be much more relevant than the hospital training I would have received.

Work was easy to find after the events I have described. It seemed that the Lord had been compelling me in that direction so that I would go to Bible College. Now I took any job I could find in order to earn money, not only to pay for my keep but also to have some in hand for the course.

Another matter began to grow in importance. Dorothy had become a State Registered Nurse and began studying midwifery. She worked long hours and then attended lectures but somehow we found time to see each other. It was often only when we met at Dudley Road Hospital gates and we went out for a walk in the park but we usually found somewhere to pray. Both of us knew that God was calling us to serve Him and we needed to be sure if we were to do this together. A decision was made and we decided to become engaged on her twenty-first birthday in October. We spent the little money we had on an engagement ring, with just enough left to buy some coffee and pay our bus fares home.

The Bible Training Institute in Glasgow, (BTI) became much more than a place of instruction to me. The austere buildings which still stand in Bothwell Street, housed not only the BTI but also the Christian Institute, used for all kinds of public meetings, and the Young Men's Christian Association, providing accommodation and recreation for many men in need. The whole complex was founded as a result of evangelistic meetings held in the city by the great American preacher, Dwight L Moody. Developed on the same lines as the Moody Bible Institute in Chicago it trained thousands of young men and women for Christian service at home and abroad.

In my time there the principal was Professor Dr Francis Davidson, DD an eminent scholar and a godly teacher. My fifth-floor room looked down upon passing trams in the noisy street below. Our compulsory quiet times were hardly quiet but nevertheless many lessons were learnt in the school of prayer and private Bible study. Here was what I had longed for, a systematic introduction to the basic doctrines of the Christian faith in fellowship with others who had heard God's call and were preparing for His service. What wonderful friendships were made, many of which have lasted for fifty years or more.

My interest in open-air preaching which I had continued even while I was in the Army caused me to be chosen as leader of the open-air team. The meetings were held on Thursday and Saturday evenings. Among crowds who thronged the main shopping area many responded to the message. In one of the streets queues of about a thousand people waited outside the Odeon cinema providing us with ample congregations. Meetings were arranged in the college for enquirers on Mondays. Other students joined us as we taught the fundamentals of the faith and discussed problems and issues. This landed me in trouble because on Monday evening the Professor gave lectures which were optional for the students but many found our meetings more attractive so we were getting more than he was! I was summoned to his office to give an account of myself and was told to keep to open-air contacts only.

On one occasion I was leading the open-air meeting and before introducing the next speaker I spoke fervently about the seriousness and urgency of the gospel message. When I had stood down I felt a tap on my shoulder and turned to be confronted by a very tall stranger. He challenged me with, 'You don't really believe all that stuff you have been saying do you?' I replied that I did and then told him a little of my story of how God had made Himself known to me and also dealt with some of his objections urging him to consider carefully the life and teaching of Jesus. As we parted he agreed that he would visit me at the college the following Monday to talk more about these things. To my great satisfaction he kept his promise. I felt somewhat inadequate to answer some of his questions. He was a middle-aged married man with a family and clearly was an honest doubter. Therefore I resorted to reading the Scriptures to him, showing him what the Lord himself said and what the Bible declared about issues he raised. As I was reading a passage from the book of Romans I glanced up and saw that tears were flowing down his face. I asked him if he believed and would like to receive Christ. He prayed openly with me confessing his sins, asking forgiveness and for the Lord to come into his life. The change that came over Jim Paisley was amazing. His natural mournful look turned into a beaming smile and for months afterwards we kept in contact. He joined his local church and became involved in Christian service.

The most dramatic event that occurred to me while I led an open-air meeting in Glasgow was as follows: In a Christian newspaper I had read an item about the holocaust. In a German concentration camp the inmates were herded together before dawn and various individuals were being selected under the pretext that they were to have a shower. Each was given a towel and piece of soap and told to join the queue. As none of the people ever returned it became evident to the rest that they were selected to die in the gas chambers. There was in this camp a Christian woman who constantly witnessed to the others about her faith in Christ encouraging them and speaking of the home in heaven which awaited them whose sins were forgiven and were trusting in the Lord. One to whom she had often spoken was a young teenage Jewish girl. On the early morning parade ground one day the teenager was selected. She was given the soap and towel and forced to join the queue that was slowly moving forward. A few moments later there was a swift movement as the Christian woman ran from the crowd, snatched the girl's soap and towel and pushed her out of the queue. A guard who saw this threatened the woman saying it was not allowed. However he relented when she pleaded for the girl's life saying, 'She's not ready yet, but I am!'

The story made a great impression upon me and I saw in it an illustration of the way Christ had died for us upon the cross. He was the substitute suffering for our sins and dying a death that should have been ours. As I was speaking at the Saturday evening open-air meeting the story came vividly to my mind and I told it to a subdued cinema crowd. There was a silent pause and then from the throng in the street to our right emerged a young woman in Salvation Army uniform. Quietly she asked if she could be permitted to speak over our microphone. Then she announced, 'The story you have been hearing is true. I am the girl who was delivered from death in the concentration camp!' Johanna-Ruth Dobschiner has since written the story in her book, *Selected To Live*[6].

The real work at BTI was of course an in-depth study of the Bible, an introduction to theology, and numerous other academic subjects that were deemed helpful for the preparation of Christian ministers and missionaries. Such studies could never be sufficient but they gave me a grounding and inspiration for which I will always be grateful.

The course was also a time for reflecting upon the call to Christian service. It was complicated however by the visits of missionaries and workers from many lands and different ministries. There were so many challenges and opportunities. But which one was the right one for us? Dorothy had become quite interested in Burma, but we learned little about that land at BTI. We discovered that two missionary societies were working there, The Bible Churchman's Missionary Society (BCMS), but we were not Anglicans, and the American Baptists. Dorothy went with me to the Baptist Missionary Society headquarters but we had no sense that God was calling us to join them.

Later while doing some personal outreach on the Glasgow streets we contacted two young foreign seamen. They accepted our invitation to an evangelistic meeting in the college. At the end they both indicated their desire to become Christians and as were soon to embark for distant lands we took the opportunity to pray with them and lead them to Christ. What a joy it was to discover that they were from Burma. One, whose name was Ha Tu corresponded with us for some time later and it was clear that he was going on with the Lord. In the end it was not for us to be missionaries to Burma but we felt that God knew the willingness of our hearts and allowed us to be a link in sending a Burmese national to carry the message to his own people.

During my time at BTI funds were in short supply. The government grant that I had received paid for the tuition and maintenance but no more. My shoes were beginning to wear out but they had not got to an emergency state when I received a caller. A young man whom I recognised as a member of the church I attended on Sunday mornings came to BTI during his lunchtime and asked to see me. He then enquired shyly about which size shoes I wore. When I told him size eight he asked if I would mind if he brought a pair for me to try on. The next day he arrived with a pair of beautiful black leather shoes. They fitted me perfectly. That was unusual because I have difficulty buying them in a shoe shop, as my feet are rather short but broad with a high instep. He then told me that he could never get shoes to fit him in a shop and therefore he had his shoes made to measure. That had happened on this occasion but even so the shoes did not fit him. I was pleased to accept them as a gift realising that the Lord had made them to measure for me. Only in that instance have I ever owned handmade shoes specially designed for me. They were the first instalment for our marriage as later that summer I wore them on our wedding day.

The early part of the summer in 1950 was glorious. A team of BTI students was invited to hold a beach mission at the popular seaside resort of Bridlington in Yorkshire. We lived in two houses made into one owned by the local Crusader youth group. The mission was an exhilarating experience as we prayed together, trusted the Lord to supply our needs, ran the children's meetings on the beach, preached on the promenade in the evenings and finally sang hymns near the harbour. At the end of three weeks we were exhausted but happy. It is difficult to measure success but in our youthful zeal we held a baptismal service in the sea for some that professed conversion.

Many years later when I was chairing a missionary meeting at which Major Ian Thomas was speaking I met a missionary whose face was familiar. We could not think where we had met before. Her missionary work was in Yugoslavia reaching into Albania which was then a strongly Marxist closed country. Eventually we realised that she had been one of those who had found Christ during our beach mission and was baptised in the sea. God encourages us from time to time by letting us know things like this but we must be patient in our ploughing and sowing with the confidence that one day we shall reap.

One week after the beach mission ended we were married. Dorothy had been nursing up until then. She was doing her midwifery course and we were delighted that news of her success came among the congratulations on our wedding day. Both being students we were short of money and our parents had little to spare though they helped as best they could. A Christian seamstress who worked in the hospital made Dorothy's wedding dress. Flowers were provided by my sister-in-law, Molly, our local church contributed foodstuffs that were still rationed. The best man's father made the three-tier wedding cake. We only had to pay for the decoration on the

top! A neighbour provided us with the wedding car and my
brother-in-law rented a cottage and a caravan for us in Wales
for our honeymoon. My cousin's husband was the
photographer. The 19th of August was a glorious sunny day,
perfect for the wedding.

For the next thirteen days it rained each day of our honeymoon. Among our wedding presents was a book entitled,
The New Testament Order for Church and Missionary by
Alex Rattray Hay[7], a missionary in South America. Looking
back I don't know how we managed it but we spent a great
deal of time during our honeymoon studying the subjects
raised in that book.

We returned to Birmingham by train almost penniless. On
arriving at Dorothy's parents' home, where we were to stay
before returning to BTI, we were greeted with the news that
they had met my cousin and that he would bring the wedding
photographs the following Monday. The next morning,
Sunday, we went to church and as we were leaving a man
gave me an envelope for which I thanked him and placed it
in my pocket. The walk from the church to the house took
about ten minutes and to our surprise there on the doorstep
was my cousin with the photographs. We went into the house
and as I had promised to pay him I went upstairs to get the
money. Of course I had nothing, but opening the envelope
in my pocket I found it enclosed just the right amount
needed to clear the debt. The Lord had known all about my
cousin coming earlier than expected and had prompted his
servant to give the right amount at the right time.

At the beginning of our married life we took seriously the
words of Jesus that we should lay up treasures in heaven, not
on earth. Certainly we had little of this world's goods. As we
did not anticipate setting up home in England we requested
that wedding presents should be in the form of money or
goods which could be used immediately or taken abroad with

us. In fact most of the money which came was used to pay college fees and obtain equipment for Dorothy to become a student at the Bible Training Institute in Glasgow. Reading through the conditions of my grant I noticed that I must notify the government of any changes in my financial situation. Considering that marriage was such a change I wrote to them saying that I had got married. To my surprise and joy they replied that that would increase the grant to provide a marriage allowance. This did not cover fees but it helped and we trusted that the Lord would pay the rest, and He did.

The college was rather Victorian in outlook. All the students were required to wear uniform that was navy blue, the women wearing broad brimmed hats. Men and women were not allowed to walk out together unless they had special permission. There were no married quarters but Dorothy and I were able to arrange that my room on the men's side be directly above her room on the women's side! She was allowed to visit my room through a connecting fire door on the second floor and later a room was put aside for married couples to use as a lounge and for making snacks on the sixth floor. Despite these restrictions we were very happy viewing them as good missionary training (GMT). Many of our fellow students became lifelong friends. They became missionaries to many parts of the world or pastors and Christian leaders at home. Dorothy had a room next to Eva's and they became firm friends. Eva later became Mrs Grogan when she married Geoffrey, the man who became a BTI student after leaving the army unit in which I also served. He continued his studies at the London Bible College and eventually became the principal of BTI, later to be known as the Glasgow Bible College, which he served for many years. Among other friendships made were that of Anne Campbell from Stornaway in the Outer Hebrides of whom mention will be made later.

A team of these students joined us at the beach mission in Bridlington in August 1951. This time I was asked to be the leader and Dorothy the cook! Geoffrey, who is a gentle giant six feet seven inches tall, played the piano accordion like a toy. He certainly attracted the children on the beach but was also an effective preacher.

John Cook was also with us. After completing his studies in London and Bristol he became an evangelist and then a much-loved Baptist minister in Gillingham, Bordesley Green, Birmingham, Surbiton and Leominster. While he was in Birmingham our friendship developed and he served the Birmingham City Mission as an adviser and representative for many years.

After the time in Bridlington the team held a mission by invitation in Quinton, Birmingham. A small church had been formed in a farmhouse under the leadership of Oliver Round. In spite of their small numbers they had a worldwide outlook. They had a special interest in overseas missions that they supported by prayer and with money. But they were also concerned about the people who lived around them in this large post-war housing suburb. One of their families was going on holiday and they allowed the team to use their beautifully furnished detached house for a team of Bible College students whom they had never met. A church member who was a grocer provided all the food each day. The team spent their time visiting the neighbourhood with Christian literature and holding all kinds of meetings in the church. There was not a great response but we learned much from the local believers about faith, prayer, generosity and godliness.

STEP SIX

Into the Market Place

It was during the next college term that we realised that Dorothy was pregnant with our first child. We were coming to the end of my course and we were praying much about our future. The mission field still beckoned us, but where were we to go? At that time we heard about the Missionary School of Medicine in London. After prayer I became convinced that it was right for us to apply. The main conditions for acceptance were that we were preparing for overseas missionary work. Normally they required that candidates were already members of a missionary society. This was not the case with us but having read our story they accepted me as a student. Again I applied for a grant on the grounds described earlier and was surprised and delighted to be given one. None of this could have happened had I not been conscripted into the army.

The college in London was non-residential so when the question of where we should live arose it was Mrs Emblen in Romford who came to our aid. She offered to let us share her home as students from Norway, Germany and China had done. It was while living there that our son David was born. Dorothy was confined to bed for three weeks before being

57

transferred to hospital for the delivery, because of serious complications. Much prayer was made and God answered by giving a normal birth.

Each day I travelled from Romford to London by train, a distance of twelve miles. Life was very hectic often standing in overcrowded London Underground trains. It was a good time to get to know people of all kinds at close quarters, but I also learned to read and study among the hustle and bustle.

Saturdays were different as the college was closed. As we did our shopping we visited the large open-air market in Romford. Thousands of people thronged the streets. The covered stalls were arranged in rows and had a vast assortment of goods for sale. Some sold books, many of which were pornographic; but there were no Christian books for sale nor any kind of Christian witness that I could see. This became a burden to me until I was pleased to hear at a combined meeting of local churches that an open-air meeting was to be held in the market place. However I was dismayed to learn that it would take place on Saturday evening. On attending I discovered that as I feared, the market place was deserted save for the Christians holding their meeting! This made me rather angry. Why didn't we try to reach the people with the gospel in the daytime when visitors came from all over Essex and elsewhere? I was then told it was against the byelaws to preach there during market hours and that the only way we could have a Christian presence there was to hire a stall.

This was a challenge to me so I felt that I should write to the town mayor stating my views and asking if we could have a Christian bookstall on Saturdays. Some days later I was invited to meet the market superintendent who told me I could have a stall on the same conditions as everyone else could. That meant being in the queue at 8.0 am, registering my name, and waiting to see if there were any vacancies. My next problem was to decide what to do. I had never sold books or taken on an enterprise like this before. Also I had little money to spare. On Monday evenings in our home at 22 The Chase, we held a prayer meeting to which about a dozen folk from different churches came. We shared the matter with them and they felt we should go ahead and they would back us up with prayer.

Next week I made my way to the Christian Literature Crusade bookshop near St Paul's cathedral and spent the small amount of money I had on books, which I believed would be suitable for sale in the market. So on the first Saturday I carried a suitcase full of books down the hill to Romford market. I was accompanied by Dorothy who in a couple of weeks later had to take to bed before the baby was born! We also took a young German lady doctor who was staying with us.

We were sorry that the only stall available was a trestle table in an open place with no covering. Soon after we had set out our books it started to rain so we used the plastic cloth which was intended to go under the books as a covering over the books. However it didn't rain for long and by the end of the day we had sold a few Christian books, given out a number of tracts and had several useful conversations sharing the gospel.

As stallholders around us were shouting about their wares I also joined in by advertising the contents of our stall and the message it contained. 'Jellied eels! All jelly!' cried the shell fishmonger. 'I'll make you a princess for seven and six', shouted the market milliner (the 'at bloke!). 'Buy one of my puppies!' called the old pet salesman. To these I now added, 'Right this way for the world's greatest book! The best book to read is the Bible!' and sometimes, 'There's something more! There's something more! There's something more than gold! To know your sins are all forgiven is something more than gold!'

There was always plenty of banter and good fun and as weeks went by we learned to love and admire many of the stallholders. They were mainly very hardworking decent people and it was a great opportunity to tell the good news of Jesus to them as well as the thousands of shoppers milling around. Each week we were given a different stall, according to what was available, and that gave us the chance to get to know many of the hundreds of stallholders. As the crowds passed along the aisles between the rows of stalls it became possible to count the visitors and estimate the total that passed by our stall in a day. It amounted to about fifteen thousand. After many months of waiting for stall vacancies at the eight o'clock rendezvous we were eventually allocated a permanent stall with its tarpaulin cover. Once there we were able to build up a group of regular customers and build up stronger relationships with them and with the surrounding stallholders. Such was the ''at bloke', the Jewish milliner who visited us in our home to enquire about the way of salvation. Many Christians came and it became an important part of the ministry to recommend appropriate books which would help them grow spiritually and inform them of the work of God outside the confines of their own church, locality and culture.

One high school girl came regularly and by this means I witnessed her grow in the Lord, go to Bible College and later heard that she went as a missionary to the Far East. Another man contacted on the stall reintroduced himself to me years later when he was the head of a large national Christian organisation. The Girls' High School was quite near the house where we were staying and Dorothy started an after school Bible class for them. By this means we got to know a number of them and exchanged greetings as they passed.

As I mentioned earlier at first we carried the books the half a mile from the house to the market place. But soon Dorothy couldn't help and no one else was available. A suggestion was made that there was an old baby's pram in the garage that might do. My pride would not allow me to walk down the street pushing a pram loaded with books and equipment for a market stall. After a while it became evident that I had no option. I felt somewhat humiliated but I consoled myself by remembering how Jesus carried a cross for me.

Then came the test. Some weeks after I had begun my weekly ordeal of pushing the pram to market and hiding it under the stall I was on my return trip heavily loaded up. I had been gradually building up the business by increasing stock and display equipment. It was an uphill push that took me passed the Girls' High School gates. On this particular Saturday there were many cars parked around the school and lots of parents were leaving. There was a special event and I arrived just as it ended. At that precise moment the axle of the pram snapped causing the contents to crash to the ground.

The pram was beyond repair so I had to ferry its contents by several return journeys from where it was to the house. At first I was deeply embarrassed but soon saw the funny side and it has given me much amusement since. The lesson that I learned was not to worry what other people think; rather it is what the Lord thinks that matters.

Our main selling was at Christmas and I was always thrilled to see Bibles and good Christian books in the hands of people who would not have thought of buying them had we not had the stall in the market place. There were some hard times, especially in the winter. It was difficult to hold on to the books when a gale was blowing. We were out there when the gales caused much flooding around the Essex coast. Many lives were lost on Canvey Island and homes destroyed on the Thames estuary. We also made wonderful friends. Harry and Doris Cross met me on the bookstall. They became prayer partners then and remain so to this day, more than fifty years later. Their periodic letters and gifts have never failed to arrive. We also met our mutual friend Michael Eastman who worked for many years for Frontier Youth Trust. When I meet him nowadays he always reminds me of our contact in Romford market.

May Gilmour used to call each Saturday morning with a flask of coffee. Then she would look after the stall for a few minutes so that I could go to the toilet. On very cold days she would take care of the stall so that I could sit somewhere in the warm to have my lunch. Such people who quietly serve the Lord in a humble way are the salt of the earth. It is difficult to recollect all the daily worthwhile and exciting events of this period nor did I keep accurate records of the amount of books I sold except Bibles of which during those five years I sold more than two thousand from the stall.

Reports of the success of the Romford Market Bible Stall got around One day I was approached by a clergyman who at the time represented the Bible Society in the district. He announced his intention to open a Bible stall for the society in the market and would I show him how it was done! He said they had money to construct a professionally built mobile stall and they already had permission from a large retail company to store the vehicle when not in use. I told him the history of my work and the hard work involved but invited him to spend a day with me. He arrived early at our home in The Chase as I packed boxes of books into a car trailer that I had acquired. Then I secured the other equipment, mounts for posters, notices and oil lamps. This heavy load I manhandled down the road while he followed at walking pace in a large expensive car behind me. When we arrived at the market he watched as I clambered around the stall erecting the display and arranging the books. Our ears rang with the shouts of the stallholders and the bustle of bringing every kind of commodity into this vast open-air market. Then came the people, not church people, or middle class well dressed and well spoken people, but the common folks who needed to look for a bargain. Many came in from the Essex countryside but there were plenty from London's East End. My visitor disappeared before the end of the day and I never saw him again. Nor did another Bible stall appear. Today Romford market is a very different place, much smaller and less busy, but not far away is a large well-stocked Christian bookshop, that some people say is the descendant of the market bookstall.

The Belhus Park Story Begins

We were excited to hear at the Monday prayer meeting that one of our members, Sidney Clark, had been preaching with two friends on the Essex village greens. On Saturday, near Aveley, they had come upon a new housing estate in the course of construction. As a few houses were already occupied the preachers began to address them. Soon they were surrounded by children who asked if they could start a Sunday school. At first the men refused saying that they lived too far away and that in any case there was nowhere for them to meet. The children urged them to come and pointed to a nearby meadow as a suitable meeting place. It was summer and the call of the children was so compelling the team agreed to come on the following Sunday. To their astonishment many children turned up. Albert Howe brought his wife to play a portable harmonium and soon the children were singing hymns and choruses in the field known as Belhus Park. They had a wonderful time and the exercise was repeated each Sunday for the rest of the summer.

It could not be expected that the fine weather would continue forever so the leaders of this new Sunday-school scouted about for any suitable building. The only one which seemed to be available was the collection of ex-army huts which were being used as canteens for the workers who were daily bussed in to build roads, services and houses. Permission was given and so the Sunday-school teachers arrived each week to dismantle tables, sweep floors, cover up obscene graffiti with Bible posters and prepare the rooms for the children. As there was little else to distract them the children arrived in hundreds. Soon there were five hundred on the books with more than three hundred attending regularly. From time to time I was invited to go over to speak to them. I was still a student at the Missionary School of Medicine living with my wife and baby David at the home of Mrs Emblen in Romford. Our interest in the new project at Belhus Park grew. We watched and prayed. My course finished in December 1952 but we still had no clear leading about the future. The missionary call had not left us and we were increasingly interested in India. Partition had recently taken place there and few in the west were aware of the horrific bloodshed or the general disruption, which had followed. Missionaries were in a very difficult situation and few societies were willing to take on young new workers. The Indian church itself wanted to distance itself from foreign influence and assert its independence.

Waiting upon the Lord for guidance regarding our future career we decided to become more involved with the Belhus Park project. As yet we were not aware of any active Christians on the housing estate so we felt that we should begin door-to-door visitation. Dorothy and I left our baby in the care of Mrs Emblen and made the ten miles journey by bus from Romford to South Ockendon, the nearest village. The rest was a matter of walking but we had to go farther on the bus to Grays in order to obtain lunch and go to the toilet. It was early in January 1953 and it was very cold. However we had some useful conversations about the gospel and distributed a fair amount of Christian literature. There was no doubt that here was a mission field where we should work for the time being.

We knocked at one door and were greeted from an upstairs window. Then the lady came down and talked to us. Her name was Mrs Ross-Watson and we engaged in an interesting conversation during which we learned that she believed in spiritualism and attended seances. Her husband, she said, was a schoolteacher and knew a lot about religion and would be glad to talk to us. We arranged to go again one evening that week.

During our visit it became clear that he too was into spiritism and would be very hard to see him delivered from it. We talked for a long time and when we were finished we had missed the last bus home. It was a cold dark winter night and we were also concerned about our baby whom we had left with Mrs Emblen in Romford. At last we began hitchhiking and were able flag down a car that took us the whole ten miles back home arriving at nearly midnight. More will be said of the Ross-Watsons later.

That same week we came across the home of George and Ella Macdonald. They were keen Christians just longing for fellowship. We were invited in and from then onwards used their home as a base where we could find shelter and eat our food. Soon we asked if we could use a room for house meetings to which they gladly agreed. They lived in a small council house in a cul-de-sac that the locals called a banjo for so it looked on the map. Our next task was to visit all the neighbours with invitations we had prepared.

Two doors away lived a lady called Doris Farrow. She agreed to come to the meeting. She listened to the Word of God and her face was radiant as she eagerly drank in the message. Later we learned that as a girl she had attended the Liverpool City Mission until the war came and she joined the Women's

Land Army. Her mother was a devout Christian who had not ceased to pray for her and now her prayers were answered. She brought her children to the Sunday school and attended the evening services, which were started in the workmen's huts. Her husband was not at all interested. He was a conductor on the London buses which meant shift work and being away from home for long hours as it was a twenty mile journey before he started collecting fares. Like most of his work mates there was little thought for religion and more interest in gambling, smoking and colourful language. At Easter he was invited to the special services we were holding but he stubbornly refused. However, by accident Doris left her Bible on the table and while she was away Stan began to read it. By the time she had returned Stan was a new man, God had met with him. Stan Farrow who served in the Marines during the war was not a man to do things by half. He threw himself into serving the Lord who had saved him. Soon he felt the conflict of the demands of his job against the time he wanted to be at church activities and studying the Bible. First he got a transfer to a local bus depot which meant less time travelling but also less money. Even then he still had to work shifts and on Sundays. It was not for legalistic reasons that he later changed his job again to drive a van delivering bread on the estate where we lived. He just wanted to be free to help in the Sunday school and use his home in the evenings for the Lord. For a number of years his home was used for the Tuesday evening prayer meetings.

The Lord honoured Stan's commitment. After we obtained a house he used to call on us on his delivery round. Always he was full of questions about his new faith. A young man was employed as his assistant and rather than seeing him sitting outside in the cold van we invited him in for a cup of coffee. He was brought up as a Roman Catholic and his brother was a priest. He too was full of questions and eventually came to a personal faith in the Lord Jesus. Later this man, Bob, married Shirley to whom I will refer later.

At the Sunday school in the huts we met one of the mothers who played the small organ for us when needed. One day I asked her if she would come to the house meetings and play for us there. Months later she told us that she had told her husband that she didn't approve of house meetings and would never let her home be used in that way. My invitation took her off guard and she agreed to come. Soon the Lord met with her. She had been brought up as a Methodist and had been active in her church in east London but she had never had a personal knowledge of the Lord. Now she experienced the joy of salvation, became a great woman of prayer, and even offered us the use of her home to start meetings for the women. Nancy Mallett became a pillar of the church, as did her husband Les who served as church treasurer and organist for many years. Their children and grandchildren are still there and have been the backbone of the youth work with the Campaigner movement.

An Angel From Iceland

Sometimes I think that the title of this book should be *'Faltering' Steps into the City*. Many times I have stumbled or been hesitant about which direction I should take. I am far from being a great man of faith but I am comforted by the story of Gideon in the book of Judges. When God called him he was in hiding from a powerful enemy. He protested to the Lord that he was weak and unfit. When eventually he made his first move he did so under the cover of darkness for fear of discovery. Then before embarking on his life work he timidly asked God to show him twice a sign in the matter of a fleece.

I am encouraged by the words of St Paul that God has chosen the weak and foolish things to serve him. It is not the greatness of our faith that moves mountains; it is a little faith in a great God.

The beginnings of a church on the new housing estate became apparent and exciting. However our eyes were upon India and we were afraid lest we should miss the way. At Easter 1953 Dorothy and I with our young baby David returned to visit our parents in Birmingham. I had an appointment in Bristol with Dennis Clarke, a missionary in India and spent a day talking and praying about the possibilities of working with him or the indigenous movement led by Bakht Singh. There was no positive outcome because of the difficult situation in the wake of partition between India and Pakistan. My letter to Bakht Singh received the reply that they were not open to young missionaries but only to mature experienced workers. It was to be another twenty-five years before I would have the joy of preaching God's word in the subcontinent. It was now three months since finishing the course at MSM. The work at Belhus was intended to be a gap-filler, serving the Lord there while awaiting an opening overseas. We were now in a dilemma. If we stayed in Birmingham we were just as likely to miss the way but where were we to go?

For some reason we had bought return rail tickets from Romford and we felt that the only course was to return. On the platform of New Street railway station in Birmingham we happened to meet Dr Julian Hoyte, a returned missionary from Africa who had conducted our wedding. He encouraged us and assured us of his prayers. We then boarded the train with our luggage consisting of two suitcases and the baby's carrycot in which David lay. We were fortunate to find an empty compartment so we placed the cot on the seat and Dorothy and I sat facing one another. The train was pulled by a steam locomotive of the Great Western Railway and consisted of carriages with compartments separated by sliding doors from the narrow corridors that ran the length of the train.

Half-way through the journey our compartment door was suddenly opened. A steward from the dining car entered and asked if we wished to buy coffee. We had brought sandwiches for the trip but had nothing to drink so we accepted the offer and the steward went away to get it. A little later he returned with a tray containing the coffeepot and cups. Just as he was arriving a very large man was moving down the corridor in the opposite direction. In order to let the steward pass the man opened our sliding door. He stepped inside to let the steward pass before realising that he also wanted to come through that door. To avoid a collision the big man sat down on the vacant seat opposite where I was with my Bible open on my lap.

The steward was paid and left us but the stranger remained. Smiling he said in halting broken English, 'You read Bible? You Christian?' I assured him that I was a Christian and asked if he was too and where he came from. He was obviously a brother in Christ and very pleased to meet me. He told me that he came from Iceland, that he was a marine engineer, and that he had been attending an exhibition at the British Industries Fair in Castle Bromwich, Birmingham. Within a few hours of having arrived in the city he had received an urgent message telling him that his mother was seriously ill and that he should return to Iceland immediately. He was now on his way to London Heathrow airport for a plane home to his city of Reykjavik. The Icelander asked me what my work was and I told him of the missionary work we had been doing in England. At this he was most interested and was full of questions about the spiritual needs of our country. After a while he stood up to leave. Taking his wallet from his pocket he produced a five pounds note, a lot of money in those days.

'When I left Iceland,' he said, 'A Christian man gave me this money to give to a Christian worker in England. You are the only Christian I meet!'

During our conversation money had not been mentioned. He had no idea that when I had paid for the coffee I had used almost all the money I possessed. God was clearly speaking to me and telling me that I was going in the right direction and that He would supply our every need. This man had spent only one night in England and was making his return journey when he met me. How was it that the sudden illness had occurred at that time? Who prompted someone in Iceland to send a gift to a Christian worker in England? How was it that the foreigner had to return home so soon and be on that particular train? Why had he been passing along the corridor at the very instant our coffee arrived! What caused me to have my Bible open upon my lap at that very moment?

It seemed to us that God had sent his angel from Iceland to confirm the way that we should go. In all my life since then I have only met one other person from Iceland.

Our First House

The distance between Romford where we were living and the estate where we were working was about ten miles. Usually we went by bus but often I cycled. On Sundays when we held a meeting in the morning, Sunday school in the afternoon and a service in the evening it meant a round journey of sixty miles. Clearly if we were to continue the work on the Belhus estate we needed to live there. The Belhus housing estate lies between the villages of Aveley and South Ockendon in the Borough of Thurrock in Essex about twenty miles east of London. About 6,000 homes were built during the time we lived there occupying about twenty-five square miles of countryside.

The Sunday school and Sunday meetings were held in the workmen's huts. The homes of the MacDonalds, Farrows and the Malletts became the centres for church activities. Although many children were coming to the Sunday school, we had no activities for them in the week. It was therefore decided to start a boys club in the Farrow's home.

We had been praying for a family of six children. The mother, Mrs Ball, occasionally came to the evening service and also to the women's meetings held at the Malletts. We were so burdened for them that one evening two or three of us spent the whole evening praying for the family Having prayed I was so convinced that this lady would become a Christian that I immediately went to the house. Although I was well received the TV was on and it was impossible to talk about anything spiritual in nature and I left somewhat disappointed. About a week or two later we commenced the boys club. That evening I set out from Romford on my bike became aware of an intensifying fog. Having cycled five miles to Upminster I realised that from then onwards it would be very dark in the country lanes. I had a dynamo lamp on the cycle but if I went too slowly it would go out. I therefore called in at the local Woolworth's and bought a torch in case. Sure enough as I cycled down the lanes it became so foggy that at one point I ran into the ditch and didn't know whether to turn left or right. I was very glad of the torch and eventually found my way to the Belhus Estate. Although the roads there were well lit the fog was very dense. It was late when I arrived at the Farrow's house and only two boys turned up. One lad lived opposite and the other lad, Terry, was the eldest boy from the family I mentioned. We played games and spent some time with the Bible.

As it was still foggy I decided to walk the boys home. When I got to their front gate I was about to say goodbye when the boy's mother appeared and invited me in for a cup of tea because it was so cold. Soon the conversation turned to spiritual things, the TV was switched off, the Bible was opened, and in an hour or so the lady was praying and asking Christ into her life. She became a truly converted Christian. The amazing thing was that when I came out of the house the fog had completely disappeared! I cycled the ten miles back to Romford in the bright light of a full moon. Here was a lesson in prayer. God always answers but in His own good time.

Not only was the travelling between Romford and Belhus

time consuming and costly, we also realised that to be effective in our ministry we needed to live among the people. In the summer of 1953 we wrote to the London County Council who owned the new houses and made an application to rent a house. Very soon we received a refusal. Some weeks later we were wearily cycling home when we passed a small derelict cottage. We looked and found it was empty. It had simply two rooms, one up and one down, and was obviously in need of repair. However, it was only half a mile from where we wished to be and we enquired at a neighbouring property as to which the owner was. We were told that it too belonged to London County Council as they had purchased the whole village. The next day we wrote to the LCC again describing the cottage and asking if we could rent it, saying we would put it in good order. This time we received a friendly letter enquiring why we were so keen to move into the area. We wrote and described the work, the hundreds of children who were coming to the Sunday-school, the meetings in various homes, and all we hoped to achieve in the neighbourhood. A few days later we heard again. We were told to go to the estate agent's office on the estate and we could choose to rent any house we wished! We knew of some houses that were just being completed and chose one of those. The paint had not quite dried!

Although we were now the proud possessors of the keys to number 25 Cullen Square we had no furniture to put in it and very little money. When we were married in August 1950 we had expected to be going abroad as missionaries. Most of our wedding presents had been money and that was spent during Bible College years. However things began to happen when Ma Emblen, with whom we were living, said that we could take the bed which we were using. Mrs Edwards, a local prayer partner offered us a table. About six pounds ten shillings came through the post that paid for four second-hand chairs and a very old three-piece suite. Stan Marshall's van was recruited to bring an assortment of donated articles from Birmingham and transport others from Romford. With these items we moved into our new house.

First we had to do the customary cleaning. We soon realised that we had no broom or cleaning materials. But there were no carpets or mats to clean, just bare tiled floors. Worse, we had no curtains to put up at the windows. Jokingly I said that we should smear whitewash on the windowpanes and pretend that we were decorating the house. I set about finding fuel for the open fireplace in the main room to dry it out.

Suddenly I heard a car draw up outside the house and looking out I saw it was an elderly couple, Bert Howe's in-laws. How wonderful they were. They said they had come to help us clean. We were amazed that they knew where we were, we hadn't told anyone. Out of the car came all the cleaning materials that we were so much in need of, then a bag of coal for the fire. Cutlery and kitchen utensils followed these, some of which we use to this day. There were also some mats for the floors. 'Now, can I put these curtains up for you?' the old man asked. I was amazed – *curtains*! He began to put them up at the main window while I got the fire going with the coal that he had brought. 'Oh, what a shame! They're too short!' he groaned. I looked for a moment and then said, 'Try another curtain. If the Lord has sent the curtains He knows the measurements and has made no mistakes.' He did. He tried another curtain and it was just the right length and he continued throughout the house. He had enough curtains for the whole house, back and front. Then he came to me in wonderment. He said,

These curtains have been stored away in a cupboard for years. We disposed of all the household effects of our mother when she died but kept the curtains. Now the problem is this, she lived in a bungalow where all the windows were the same height. How is it that they all fit your windows perfectly when your bedroom windows are shorter than the windows downstairs?

The Lord knew. The new house became a centre for Christian life and outreach. Contact was made with another family in Cullen Square where there was an interest in spiritual things. Their boy, David Coles, came regularly to the boys club that was started at Number 25. He later became a wonderful Christian man and a leader in the church. He married Carol, daughter of the caretaker of a school in which we held a Sunday school. We went there because the caretaker of another school we used refused to have us there any more. How God so wonderfully works for good!

The people next door must have thought that we were very rich. Often they would call to see if they could borrow something. Usually it was for money in order to pay the fare for their daughter to work on Monday morning or for a packet of tea or sugar. There was never a time when we were unable to meet their need. Little did they know that the only regular income we were receiving was a child allowance of five shillings per week. All other money came by gifts from friends and supporters, mainly by post. The only way we solicited these gifts was by prayer to our Heavenly Father.

At the eastern side of Cullen Square is a small piece of wild countryside sloping down to the Mar Dyke. The children loved to play there hiding from one another among the hawthorn and broom bushes. When David was three or four he became the proud owner of a cowboy outfit (no gun!) One day he returned home crying. He had lost his cowboy belt somewhere among the shrubbery near the Mar Dyke. Now there was a lot of shrubbery and to find a small brown belt was like looking for a needle in a haystack. Moreover there were many children playing there and some would take such a belt from your own property let alone leave a spare one lying on the ground. Finders were keepers!

In such small incidents lessons can be learned. We wiped away David's tears and then turned to the Lord in prayer asking Jesus to help us find the belt. Together we went back to the playing area and within a few minutes we found there hanging on a bush, within everyone's sight, was the cowboy belt. How happy we were to return home and thank the Lord for His help.

To help out with expenses Dorothy was able to do some part-time district nursing. That opened many homes for us including one where an old lady was dying of cancer. Dorothy nursed her to the end and used to take with her copies of the *Christian Herald*. By this time I was building up a list of people who were willing to take this paper weekly and I used to deliver them. Many were the good conversations we had at such times

After the old lady died her daughter was happy to continue to receive the *Christian Herald*. One day I knocked at their door her son, a bright fourteen-year-old boy answered. As he took the paper I asked if he was in any boys organisation or if he went to church, Sunday-school or Bible class. When he answered in the negative I asked if he would like to go to a boys' Bible class. He said that he would. I did some quick thinking and invited him to come to one in my home. The next Sunday afternoon he attended and he was the only boy!

This was the beginning of our boys' club that was to reach many boys and their families in the days ahead. Victor Parsons, the boy in question, later became a fine Christian man. His wife Barbara also came to Christ indirectly as a result of our door-to-door visitation. Together they have run youth activities, camps and house parties reaching hundreds of young people in Essex, Kent and Surrey. They have served as deacons and leaders in their local churches and using their home as a centre of Christian testimony.

The Right Place

We had moved to Belhus to continue planting a new church. This we did by making the good news of Jesus known by all means. The chief means was door-to-door visitation that was very hard. People were naturally suspicious and often resented leaving their newly acquired black and white television to talk about religion. Some days we could see little fruit for our labours.

One morning Ma Emblen came to baby-sit for us so that Dorothy and I could go out on the doors together. I remember praying, Lord, let us hear your voice saying, 'Put your nets out on the right side of the ship for a draught of fishes'. It was then decided that we should visit a newly occupied block of flats. We took with us Gospels of St John. Our usual approach was to welcome the newcomers to the estate and offer help if they needed it. We then asked if they had a copy of the Bible in their new home. If they had not we then offered a free copy of a portion of it in the form of John's Gospel. That day a few of these books were given away but otherwise it was unremarkable.

'Have I come to the right place?' The speaker was a small wizened old lady, poorly dressed and with a rather squeaky

Army training

Faith wedding, 19th August 1950

Romford market stall, 1954

The Missionary School of Medicine in 1952

At our new house –
25 Cullen Square, 1953

First Sunday School in Belhus Park,
August 1951

David the young preacher

Rainbow circle near Cullen Square

Children's Open Air at Kingshurst, 1964

Covenanters at 46 Wheeley Moor Road, 1965

Sunday School at Overgreen Hall, 1963

Washington Court Opening, 1995

Edwin R. Orton

Don Maclean and Martin Hone at hostel opening, 1995

Silver Jubilee celebration, 1991

Kingshurst Evangelical Church, 2005

voice. I say she was old but that was not really true. She looked old, her face bearing the signs of neglect, abuse and alcohol, her hair unkempt, thin and prematurely grey.

She held in her hand a small yellow book bearing the letters SGM. I recognised it immediately as we had distributed many copies around that new London housing estate. The Scripture Gift Mission had generously supplied these copies of the Gospels for our work in planting a new church in a needy area of Essex. On numerous occasions we found that the simple story of Jesus and the words which he uttered had produced a profound effect upon the readers.

'Yes, you are in the right place,' I answered, seeing as she turned the book over in her hands that our address was printed on the back. 'Good' she continued, 'Then I want you to tell me what has been happening to me.'

Dorothy and I invited her into our new but sparsely furnished council house. Soon she was seated and over a cup of coffee told us her story. Helen Chunn had had a very hard life. There was nothing that she knew about her father. Her childhood was spent in a poor house in London's East End with her mother who made her living from the numerous boyfriends who visited the house. One was a kind of stepfather who looked after the money. Until she was ten Helen was the only child, unwanted, neglected and rejected. Most of the time she kept out of their way, glad enough to have something to eat and a place to sleep.

Then her mother had another baby. She remembered the rows and the fights. They didn't want a baby and the pregnancy was treated as a crime against the family. How could she earn her living in that condition? The days and nights grew quieter, but there was hunger and cold, and even more neglect. When the baby arrived there was little excitement, but rather fear and foreboding. The tired mother was sick, weary and sad. Helen had to do the chores, fetching and carrying and trying to prepare what little food was available. The months that followed hung as a cloud in the memory of this woman as she told her story. Her mother's sickness grew worse. The baby was often crying and Helen spent the nights trying to pacify her before she herself fell into exhausted sleep.

One morning Helen's mother would not awaken. She lay very still, cold and pale. What was the poor girl to do? The baby was crying and there was no food in the house. Helen ran to the neighbours shouting and screaming for help. Soon a group of women, much like her mum, were crowding her doorway. People were coming and going, policemen and doctors. Helen hid in the crowd. She noticed a woman in nurse's uniform carrying the baby out of the house.

Afraid that they would take her away too Helen ran away. She knew a few of her mother's friends who lived a mile or so away. They had their own reasons why they should avoid the police and other authorities. They took Helen in and she felt secure. They also gave her food and a bed. By the time Helen was twelve she was expected to earn her living. At those times there was a demand for the services of young girls and Helen soon learned the horror of being mauled and abused. There was that artificial atmosphere of friendliness and hollow affection that was contrived to attract the clients, but she herself experienced the fear and revulsion of reality. Yet it was a living. But the years of poverty and depression in the early thirties made the trade of prostitution highly competitive. Other means of earning money needed to be found. Petticoat Lane was the most famous of London's street markets. There and in similar places Helen learned the art of stealing purses and handbags. The associate who stalked her prey would never actually take the goods but simply mark the victim for another. Once the bag was taken it was to yet another associate and finally one more.

It was not always so successful. As the crowds pushed their way down the narrow lanes between the market stalls there were policemen and women in plain clothes that constantly scrutinised the passers-by for furtive behaviour. Helen described to us her own emotions as like a hunted fox when she had been sighted and chased still clutching the stolen purse. Not only the police but the crowds of shoppers had turned upon her. Blindly she fled from the deafening cries and shouts of her pursuers turning sharply through a gap in the stalls to enter a side street. To her horror it was a blind alley. There was no way out. Like a pack of hounds her assailants were upon her. She lay trembling and afraid until she was dragged roughly to her feet by the strong representation of the law. It was the beginning of Helen's life of crime and punishment.

We listened that sunny spring morning as to some female Ancient Mariner who held us with her glittering eye. The stories tumbled out, of pain and shame, villain and victim. The first taste of imprisonment removed from her whatever vestige remained of innocence and pride. She had embarked on an unforgiving life of vice and crime.

Just when all seemed lost to the inevitable squalor and disease of the streets a ray of hope arrived in the form of a client who took a fancy and then really fell in love with her. The tall Canadian swept Helen off her feet with stories of wealth and adventure in his vast North American country. He offered to marry her and she grasped the opportunity for deliverance. For a while she was very happy living in the new house her husband built for her. But this was a new world with wide-open spaces and few people. Those she met were of a different class and she was constantly embarrassed because of her lack of education and inability to communicate. She missed the hustle and bustle of the big city and the life style she was used to. Soon she became irritable and restless and there were rows between her and her husband.

Early one morning she packed her things and any money she could lay her hands on and left, heading for the USA. She crossed the border without difficulty and sought work in the nearest big city. Helen's self reliance stood her in good stead for a while as she found a place to live and worked in a local factory. However she needed more money and started stealing again. When she was arrested it was discovered that she was an illegal immigrant. The police contacted her husband at her last known address in Canada but he had had enough and refused to take her back. Ellis Island near New York, the detention centre for those people awaiting deportation, became her home. In disgrace Helen Chunn arrived by ship at Liverpool docks. She described her feelings as she stepped on to the quay penniless and with only a small bundle of clothing thrown after her. It was a long and painful journey, but she determined to return to London the city of her birth and she walked most of the way.

But the war had changed everything. The bombing of the East End had destroyed whole streets and removed landmarks. The work of demolition and rebuilding was in full swing. All her old haunts had disappeared and the familiar faces had gone. Not only so, but she herself had changed. Her life of prostitution had caused premature ageing and it showed in her face. No one wanted her. She had never heard of the welfare state and the assistance the government offered. Her only resort was begging and picking up other peoples leftovers, a typical vagrant 'bag lady'. Relief was only to be found at soup kitchens and in charity night shelters. Stress and strain and lack of food took their toll and finally she was found lying in the street unconscious.

How long she was there or how long she lay in hospital she did not know but when she did recover the problem was to find her a place to stay. The doctors warned that if she returned to the streets of London she would die. At last she was offered a flat on a new housing estate. It was at the door of that flat that Dorothy and I had knocked one bright morning and offered her the yellow covered gospel of St John. It was not the end of the story. Helen had found the right place. We were able to share with her in word and deed the love that God had for her. She drank in the word of God; soon reading from cover to cover the Bible we gave her. It took her some time to accept that she could be forgiven.

When I visited her flat I found that the only furniture she had was a bed and a gas stove which she never used. She said that she had been so wicked that she felt the stove would explode in her face if she lit it! We saw the change which Christ alone can make in a life so ravaged by sin. She told us that the reason she came to us in the first place was that that very morning she had asked her neighbour if she could get anything from the shops for her. When she moved in to her flat she had been rude to the neighbour not wanting anything to do with her. 'What has happened to me?' she asked, 'It's something to do with this book!'

A couple of years later Helen moved back to London into another flat of her own. I visited her on two occasions, one was in summer and I noticed that a Christmas card we had sent was still on the mantle shelf. It was the only one she had received and it was treasured. Later I learned that she told her new neighbour that her son had been to see her!

God Answers

'Ross-Watson from South Ockendon' is not a title to be easily mistaken, not like John Brown of London or Mary Jones of Cardiff. It was in the early 60s that WEC acquired their splendid headquarters at Bulstrode in Buckinghamshire. We had taken a coach party from Birmingham to the opening event that included a valedictory for new missionaries. One was going to Indonesia. He gave his testimony, which sounded familiar to me, and then said he was Michael Ross-Watson from South Ockendon. Afterwards we compared notes and he cried, 'So you're the man who used to call at our house'.

I have mentioned that first day of visitation in January 1953 when on a cold winter's morning we knocked at a door and were greeted from an upstairs window. After our first evening revisit we had to hitchhike back to Romford! For three years we continued to visit that family, the Ross-Watsons. Always we could talk. They were intelligent well-read people who were interested in religion but committed to 'spiritualism'. No way would they come to any of our church meetings and they resolutely refused to allow their children to attend our Sunday school. They did accept our weekly edition of *Christian Herald*. Three years after our first meeting they moved house. As they were still on the Belhus, South Ockendon estate I found their address and continued to visit them for another year. One sunny Saturday morning Mr Ross-Watson was working in his garden when I arrived.

'You're wasting your time coming here', he said, 'We are not coming to your church, we're not sending our children to you, and we don't want any more of your literature, so please don't come again.'

I was disappointed and told him that we had prayed for them over the years and although we would visit no more if that was what they wished we would nevertheless continue to pray. This we did from time to time. Soon we ourselves moved to Kenningtons estate and later on to Birmingham.

Michael told us his story of the intervening years. He remembered our visits and the literature we took to his house. Some years later his father invited him to attend some meetings arranged by students from Cliff College, Calver, near Sheffield. Mr Ross-Watson was a teacher and the school secretary, who he much respected, had invited him and his family to an event at her Methodist Church. The church was noted for its social activities so they didn't expect an evangelistic rally.

The students were lively and cheerful, and full of enthusiasm for the good news of Jesus. It struck a chord in Michael's heart as he listened to the message with gladness. He persuaded his father to let him go to the rest of the meetings. At last the teenager committed his life to follow Christ.

After the students had left Michael began to attend the Methodist church but this one was liberal and Michael's hunger and thirst for God was not being met. He remembered the church that was being founded when we used to visit and started to attend that. As he studied the Bible he saw the need for believer's baptism and asked to be baptised by immersion in water. His father was so angry with this that he turned him out of the house. Cliff College students had kept in touch with Michael and when they heard what had happened he was invited to the college. Soon he became a student himself and later a full-time evangelist on the staff. It was there that he heard God's call to missionary work in Indonesia. He applied to the Worldwide Evangelistic Crusade (WEC) and after a period of training at their headquarters was ready to leave for the field. 'My name is Michael Ross-Watson and I come from South Ockendon in Essex!'

It was a privilege some years ago to have the now well known missionary, Bible teacher and conference speaker, Michael Ross-Watson, to be our guest at the Birmingham City Mission annual conference.

Faith Tested and Rewarded

In the summer of 1953 when we were commuting between Romford and South Ockendon our friends George and Ella MacDonald who were the first Christian believers we had met on that estate made a generous offer to us. As they were going on holiday for two weeks they said that we could live in their home while they were away. We knew that they were not well off financially, he being a bus conductor, so we accepted their kind offers on condition that we paid the rent for the house while they were away. Not far from the house in Loman Path where we lived for those two weeks was a small shopping centre in front of which was a wide grassy area. We decided to hold some meetings for children on the green. Many came because they got so bored during the long holidays and their mothers were glad for some respite. The meetings were run in the fashion of the beach meetings held at Bridlington. Music was provided by my limited skills on an old concertina we had been given. They were great fun and resulted not only in the children learning wonderful Bible stories and great Christian songs but also giving us contact with new families. I believe this may be where we met the child of Mary Ellis whom I will mention shortly.

All our funds at that time had to come in answer to prayer. No one was paying us and we had no money in the bank. Occasionally someone would pass on a gift to us by hand. Sometimes we would receive a letter containing money through the post. Now we were to be put to the test.

Monday had arrived, the day that the rent collector would call. We literally had no money at all, we had managed the weekend shopping but now there was nothing to pay the rent.

As usual we gave ourselves to prayer. God had not failed us in the past and we were sure He would not fail us now. But nothing happened. No visitors came and no post arrived. We prayed again!

Looking out of the window we saw the rent man going around the banjo (the local name for the cul-de-sac). We heard his footsteps going to the house on our left followed by the knock on their door. I took out the rent book from the electric meter cupboard beside the front door and held it in my hand. How would I explain our lack of money? The footsteps receded from our neighbour's door but then passing our house they proceeded to the door of the house on our right!

In astonishment I opened the rent book I was holding. There, to my amazement I found that the MacDonalds had, despite our agreement, already paid the rent.

That was the only time during that period that it seemed that God had failed – and He had not. The rent had been paid for one week only. When the rent man called the following week and knocked our door we had the money to pay!

We learned another lesson from this incident. God's word makes it clear that we are all in debt to Him because of our sin. How can we pay that debt? All our good works are not enough to cover the sins we have committed in thought, word and deed. Our situation is desperate. But what we need to do is to look into the Book. The Bible reveals that Christ died to pay the debt of our sins. If we put our trust in him we will be set free from the debt we could never repay by ourselves.

*　　*　　*

In the spring of 1956 I was invited to be among the speakers at a missionary conference at The Longcroft at Barnston in the Wirral, Cheshire. The meetings were to begin on Monday so I felt that I should travel from our home in South Ockendon, Essex on Saturday and spend the weekend with our parents and home church in Birmingham through which I would pass on the way. Saturday was the day on which I continued to hold a Bible Bookstall in Romford market place. I planned to begin my journey from there to Birmingham after the stall closed at six in the evening.

We were very short of money at that time. In our work of planting a church on the Belhus Park estate we received no salary and had no other regular income. The Lord was our employer so our trust was in Him so we prayed hard and lived on what was given in kind or arrived by post from interested friends.

On that Saturday morning we had no money apart from my bus fare from home to Romford. It was not easy to pack my bag and leave Dorothy, my wife, with two small children, and Anne Campbell, our fellow worker, with no money and little food in the house. About an hour later I arrived at The Chase where my stock of books was kept. I then loaded the trailer and manhandled it the half-mile down hill to the market where I set up the stall for the day.

As usual it was a busy day with up to fifteen thousand shoppers jostling past the stall in the large open market straddling the London Road. About everything you could think of was sold there; farm produce, groceries, clothing, household goods, animals, works of art and of course my

Christian books and Bibles. It always brought me great joy when I sold a Bible or some other Christian book to someone who was just passing by with no thought of God until being attracted to the stall. The stall was well decorated with bright posters displaying challenging Scripture texts. It stood out among other stalls that claimed attention by appealing to baser instincts.

Sales were never high except just before Christmas. On this occasion they were not great but the takings were sufficient for me to buy a single rail ticket from Romford to Birmingham. I made the journey late that evening first to Liverpool Street in London, then by underground to Paddington and finally by express steam train to Snow Hill, Birmingham. By the time I paid the bus fare from the city to Yardley where I was to spend the night I had only a few pence in my pocket. How I was to pay for the rest of the journey north I did not know but my trust was in God. Over many years it had been our practice to tell no one but God about our financial needs and this I continued to do.

The following morning I went with Mr and Mrs Perkins, my wife's parents, to the service at the Gospel Hall, our local chapel. The friends were surprised to see me and made me welcome. Afterwards one of the elders who did not expect to see me and who knew nothing of my circumstances and rarely gave me anything placed an envelope in my hands. Later when I opened it I was overjoyed to find enough money to pay my fare as far as the conference in the Wirral.

The invitation to the missionary conference came through Albert MacDowell, a missionary returned from Brazil. As Home Secretary for his mission he had visited us in Essex and wanted me to share my experiences with people who would pray for us. He was recovering from a traumatic event in the Amazon jungles in which all his mission station colleagues had been massacred and he had been the lone survivor. While serving in a remote jungle mission station he had been engaged with others learning unknown tribal languages and putting them for the first time in written form. Then would follow Bible translation and a literacy programme.

Unfortunately a Portugese telegraph engineer who had influenza had been installing equipment passed on the infection to local native Indians who had no resistance to the virus. The disease spread rapidly among the villagers with fatal results. It was as if a plague had struck. Gradually the survivors believed that their calamity was associated with the intrusion of the white man whom they thought must have brought evil spirits.

Albert was the youngest of the small missionary group and the only single man. It was his duty to make the journey lasting several weeks through the forest to collect supplies from the nearest town. Travelling by mule and canoe was an exhausting and dangerous occupation. On this occasion when he returned to his horror he found that the mission station had been ransacked and the murdered bodies of the missionaries and their children were lying about the camp. The young man was left alone to bury the dead, close down the station and carry the disastrous news back to the outside world.

At the missionary conference at The Longcroft I felt honoured to be with Albert MacDowell and a number of other missionary warriors. During one of the sessions an elderly couple were introduced to us as retired missionaries from Bolivia, Mr and Mrs Thomas Easdale. Although in their late seventies they assured us that they were not retired but in fact had a passage booked to return to Bolivia where God had called them many years before. They had been successful in planting many churches in that country and in Argentina[8]. On the morning of our departure from the conference in the Wirral, Mr Easdale took me aside and told me that the Lord had indicated to him that he should make me a gift of money.

I found it hard to believe that such a person would be the means by which my needs would be supplied. We travelled together to Liverpool and parted at Pier Head before I found the railway station and bought my ticket back to Romford. The gift was more than enough!

When I left home I knew there were no funds and there was little food in the house. At that time we had no telephone so there were no means of communication while I was away, all I could do was to pray for those I had left behind. Eagerly on my return I wanted to know how the family had fared.

On the Saturday I left there had been no postal gifts. There had been enough food for meals that day but no money to buy any more. After breakfast on Sunday the cupboard was bare. It was Dorothy's turn to attend morning worship in the huts that served as our church building and Anne's turn to look after the children. They both hoped that there would be no visitors. Often one of the nurses who was off duty would be invited to lunch. To Dorothy's horror there was one in the service and she asked if it was all right for her to come home. When they arrived they could smell cooking. Anne had found some vegetables and herbs in our out-house, and had somehow made an appetising meal. Nothing was said about the financial situation but after the nurse had left to go on duty they discovered that she had left an envelope for them containing enough money for a week's shopping. However it was Sunday and even if the shops had been open they would not have gone to them on the Lord's day.

In the late afternoon they were faced with the dilemma of having no food at all in the house. What should they do? They left it in the Lord's hands and laid the table for tea. Just at that moment they looked out of the window and noticed a car draw up. To their dismay they saw it was a family from Romford whom we had recently counselled as new Christians.

Weeks ago they had been invited to call on us for tea yet this was their first visit.

When the Quinlans entered the room where the table was laid but with no food they said, 'Oh! Are we too late, have you already eaten?'

When Dorothy told them they were just getting ready for a meal Doris replied, 'Good because we have bought some goodies for you!'

She then returned to the car and produced a hamper bulging with food of every kind down to the smallest detail to make a sumptuous meal. God had honoured His promise once again!

How we rejoiced as we compared notes regarding His testing and provision during that week in which we had been apart. We had not only survived but were better off than when I left, and more importantly we had learned deep lessons in the life of faith.

On many occasions during that period of our lives we were severely tested and yet found that the Lord was faithful and he provided for us. Christmas time was especially difficult. There were times when we were so short of money that when Dorothy went to do her shopping she would look in the shop window at the prices and work out what she could buy with the money in her purse before she entered. Sometimes when we returned home we found groceries on the doorstep and to this day we don't know who put them there. Also it was a total stranger who knocked on our door and handed in a large turkey ready for our Christmas dinner.

One day we were particularly tested, as after breakfast we had no food in the house and no money. We spent time in prayer but even so I felt rather depressed and disinclined to go visiting from door-to-door. However I felt drawn towards a new housing area that had recently been inhabited. After a while of knocking doors, welcoming the residents and speaking to people about the Lord I came across a tall elderly lady. She expressed great pleasure in meeting me for she said she was a believer, lived alone and had been in her flat for several weeks but had not found a church. She invited me in and soon we were talking about the things of God and I encouraged her with words from the Bible. Then we prayed together and I got up to leave.

'Just one moment' she said, and going into another room she returned with a small box. 'I told you that I haven't been able to go to church since being here' she confided, 'but I have been putting aside the money I usually put in the offering. I want you to take it and use it as you will.'

At no point had I mentioned money to her or given her the slightest indication of our needs. God knew and he had led me to this lady whom he had prepared and through whom he fulfilled his promise to us, 'My God shall supply all your needs according to his riches in glory by Christ Jesus' (Phil 4:19). We received sufficient funds for food for the day and for the week ahead.

Visitation Stories

An important aspect of visitation was to follow up children who were absent from Sunday school. One boy who had been absent for a few weeks was found to be suffering from a broken leg received in collision with a motor car. We visited him several times and on each occasion talked to his mother. She was interested in the Christian message. At that time her husband, Will Barcham who was a construction engineer, was working away in Canada. But one day when we called he met us at the door and invited us in. Now he was home he said he would like to attend our church that was still meeting in the workmen's huts. However he would wait till the eldest boy was old enough to care for the rest of the children before he came. It was perhaps two years later that a couple turned up at our evening service. They were vaguely familiar. Then they reminded me of their promise. Clive, their eldest son, had had a birthday and they decided he was old enough to be in charge of the children while they went to church. I was amazed because so many people had made promises to come but never did. Here were quality folk who not only attended but also were eager to find out what it was all about.

It was not long before they were baptised and active members in the church. Will hired the gymnasium at the Culverhouse school in order to run a boys' club. He was a large athletic man who was also deeply spiritual and he became a strong influence for good in the lives of many of the lads. They eventually moved to the west country where they served the Lord faithfully. For many years they kept in touch with us and supported us by prayer and financially through all the early years after we moved to Birmingham.

One day I received a most interesting letter. It was from a bus driver who lived in Darren Drive on the Belhus estate. He had received a leaflet through his door and was interested to learn more about the Christian life. I arranged to visit him and found him to be a very tall quiet serious minded Londoner.

He told me that he used to receive tracts like the one I had pushed through his door from a colleague, who had passed on these Christian leaflets from time to time. He had read them with interest. Finally he had decided that he wanted to become a Christian and so looked out for his friend for help. Usually they met in the staff canteen between shifts. This was a haphazard arrangement as shifts varied and were subject to change. However, months passed without them meeting so my friend went to the general office and asked for the man's address. He was told that the driver no longer worked for them because he had emigrated to Australia.

Since then he had been without any contact with a Christian and waiting for an opportunity to become one. Then the tract arrived on his doormat. I asked him how long he had been waiting. He replied, 'Ten years!' It was my joy to explain the gospel to him and invite him to receive Christ that he did eagerly. He became a regular attendee at our church meetings but his wife was reluctant to come. She had been brought up in the Church of England and had no wish to join a non-conformist free church, as she saw it. Wisely the converted driver took her to a Church of England where she could hear the word of God. They became active members of that church.

From these events I learned many lessons. One was that the man who gave out tracts had been sowing good seed and although he perhaps never heard of the results there had been fruit in the end. I learned too the value of persevering. On the day I put the tract through the door I had been knocking doors and speaking to the people. There had been a poor response but when no one answered I had posted the leaflets through the letterbox. Another lesson was not to be bothered about recruiting for our own church. Our business is to preach Christ and He, the Good Shepherd, will take care of His sheep.

The leaflet that had aroused the attention of the bus driver was entitled, *Swimming Against the Stream*. It was produced by The Evangelical Tract Society, which was based at that time in Harrow. I wrote to the General Secretary, Eric Williams, and told him of the man's conversion. This began a lasting friendship and later a strong partnership between ETS and the Birmingham City Mission. On numerous occasions I drove to their headquarters and was provided with thousands of gospel tracts. When I protested that we could not afford to buy them Eric would tell me that he would trust the Lord with me. He maintained that as long as he gave out tracts freely sufficient gifts came in but when he tried to balance the budget by selling them he was in financial difficulties. Eric Williams was a real man of faith and prayer and a great encourager. Since his Home Call we have missed him very much.

Our Sunday evening services were being held in the workmen's huts. I arrived just as it was getting dark and I noticed the figures of a man and a boy crossing the road. The boy disappeared inside the hut but the man re-crossed the road and went away into the darkness. On entering the hut I noticed the boy sitting alone as one of our Sunday-school children. He was a pleasant intelligent lad who was always keen to ask and answer questions in class. After the service I chatted with him and found that he had persuaded his father to bring him to the service though he himself did not stay. I later met his father and told him that when the boy came to the service I would make sure that he got home safely.

When I visited the boy's home and met his mother the children were well clothed, fed and well behaved. She was glad that the Sunday school was near to them and made sure that her children attended regularly. Mrs Cordier was obviously a very caring mother. Having a copy of the *Christian Herald* with me I passed it on to her.

On another occasion I called again and asked if she had enjoyed reading the paper I gave her and if she would like to receive it regularly. She willingly agreed and so she became one of my weekly contacts of which I had about seventy at that time. One beautiful spring morning I met Mrs Cordier at her garden gate. We talked about the contents of the *Christian Herald* and then on to the way of salvation. At that point I produced a copy of the Scripture Gift Mission Gospel of St John. At the back of the book was a decision statement that read,

> Being convinced that I am a sinner and believing that Christ died for my sins and rose again from the dead I now receive him as my personal Saviour and Lord and by his help intend to follow Him.

I asked her if she had ever received Christ in that way. To my surprise she said that she had. 'When was that?' I asked. 'Just now, as you read that page to me' she replied.

She then invited me into her house so that I could pray with her and explain more fully the first steps in the Christian life. When I was finished she went out into the kitchen and produced a huge box of cigarettes. 'For years I have been a chain-smoker, and these have kept me from coming to the Lord. Now that I have received Him I will no longer need them!'

With that she went outside to the refuse bin, broke up the cigarettes, and threw them in. From that day onwards she never smoked again. Mrs Cordier became a devout member of the church, regularly attending the services and living an exemplary Christian life. For many years, after the family moved from the estate, she kept in touch as a prayer partner.

Visitation does have its tough side. So often people just don't want to know. They are suspicious and afraid. Door-to-door salesmen, religious cults and press reports of con men and violent crime make some folk, especially the elderly, afraid to open their doors to strangers. It is important to understand that their fears are well founded and to take care not to scare them and show that our intention is to do them good. On one occasion I called on a frail elderly couple who were very wary. They had not long moved into their ground floor maisonette. I did my best to allay their fears by telling them who I was, where my family lived, and where the local shops and services were. Finally I asked if there was anything practical I could do to help them. With that he escorted me round to the back of the house and showed me their garden! It was just a mass of weeds. After that it was my weekly duty to spend a few hours taming the wilderness and making it a place for the old couple to sit in comfort.

Their fears had gone and I was always invited into the house for a cup of tea. Soon we were reading the Bible together and answering their questions. Not only so but their neighbours were told and our visits turned into a weekly house-group.

The Billy Graham evangelistic crusades in Harringay and

Wembley, London, provided a great opportunity for visitation on the Belhus estate. I had heard Billy Graham and his song leader Cliff Barrows on their first visit to Britain in 1946. A meeting was held for them in the Friends' Institute, Moseley, in Birmingham. When they came to London I determined to take coach parties to the meetings. We had some invitations printed and I went round to my contacts asking them to come.

Mary Ellis had started attending some ladies meetings held in various homes. She had become one of my *Christian Herald* readers and agreed to come to Wembley to hear Billy Graham. How we prayed for her. Mary had been brought up in a Roman Catholic family and attended a Roman Catholic school. She had had some bad experiences there and had decided to give religion a miss altogether. But God had awakened her. That meeting night was cold and wet, nevertheless seventy thousand people crowded into the great Wembley football stadium to hear the American evangelist. They did so each night for a week. We were fairly high up, a long way from the pitch but we heard the massed choirs clearly, joined in the singing, were moved by the solos of Beverley Shea and enthralled by the preaching of Billy Graham. At the invitation there was a calm silence. No one seemed to move, and then just here and there an individual left his seat and moved towards the arena. Gradually the trickle became a stream. One of our coach party stood and went down the aisle, then another. Behind us were a group of soldiers, guardsmen doing their annual duty at the Royal Barracks. There had been some coarse remarks from that area but now all was quiet. Suddenly two of them stood up and strode down the long aisle to the football pitch which had now become crowded with men and women, young and old who had responded to the invitation to receive Christ as their own personal Saviour. Each person was counselled and received helpful literature. It was an amazing sight to see so many making their stand for Christ. They came from all sections of society, denominations, races and religions.

Mary Ellis did not go forward. There was no pressure. It took some time for us all to get back on the coach; a number clutching the literature they had received. As it was late we only sang a little on our way home. Some were very joyful, others just thoughtful.

Next day it was time to deliver the *Christian Herald* newspapers and I called on Mary. When I asked what she thought of the Wembley meeting she told how she wished she had gone forward. I asked why and it became clear that she had understood the gospel message and had a genuine desire to become a Christian. When I told her that she did not need to be in a big meeting to make a decision like that she invited me into her home. The Bible was opened and the way of salvation explained again. We prayed together and she invited the Lord Jesus Christ to be her Saviour and Lord. She has followed the Lord for almost half a century and has been leader of the Ladies' meeting in her church for many years.

'God Taught Me to Read'

'Ah, There you are. I'm glad I got here before you went away.' These were the words with which the old lady greeted me at the gate of a country cemetery on a snowbound day in February 1955. I had just conducted a funeral in this place, a mile or so from the village. The bus had taken me to Rainham in Essex and I had walked the rest in several inches of snow. The mourners had arrived in limousines with the Daimler hearse. The service was held on the unheated chapel and we had trudged through the snow to the open grave for the committal. No one wanted to stay for long and soon the small crowd was gone and I was left alone.

'I was doing my ironing when the Lord said to me, "Go and take that lad a warm drink"!' On the previous Sunday it had been announced in her church that a funeral was to be held and that I would be conducting it. Neither the information nor the subsequent change in the weather had escaped her notice.

It was clear that this seventy-eight year old lady had tramped from the village through the snow but she made nothing of it. She urged me to return to the chapel to avoid the bitter biting wind. Soon we were sipping hot coffee that she had brought in a flask. Sitting in that cold chapel she quietly told me her story.

Ironing was one of the chores that she did for her invalid husband who had been bed-ridden for more than seven years. She undertook her task cheerfully, but it was also her place of prayer. Strange how an ironing board can be changed into an altar! There were plenty of people to pray for. There she also meditated on her morning Bible readings and prepared for the ladies meetings she was invited to address from time to time in neighbouring villages. Then there were her own missionaries!

Country life had been hard when she was a girl. Poverty made school out of the question and drove her to work in the fields at an early age. Not that she had been unhappy for she loved nature and the open air.

Sunday was always special to her as that was the day she did not work the long hours and when she could be with her friends at the local Free Church. How she enjoyed the singing and listening to the stories of Jesus. A special treat was when a missionary told of his exploits in Africa, India or China. She yearned to go out there herself but that was impossible. But she could pray.

One Sunday, when she was in her early teens her Pastor spoke to her in the chapel as she was leaving the morning service. 'We are in need of another Sunday-school teacher,' he intimated, and I wonder if you would consider taking on the task.'

That had been a day of great excitement for her, but one of acute embarrassment. At that moment there was nothing else she would rather do than to teach children the love of Jesus but the plain fact was that not having been to school she herself could neither read nor write. What was she to do? Most people in the church, including the Pastor, didn't know. She always carried a Bible to church and appeared to use the hymnbook. Actually she had memorised most of the hymns by listening to others and singing them over and over again in the fields as she worked.

When Mary reached home she quickly went to her room and fell on her knees. There she poured out her problem to God in prayer tearfully asking for His help. The answer came speedily. The Lord would teach her to read. At church that day someone had helped her find the place in the Bible from which the reading was taken. There was still a marker in the place. Nervously she found the place again and tried to remember some of the words spoken by the reader. To her joy she discovered that she could recall some and fit them to the characters on the printed page of her King James Version of the Bible.

From then onwards each Sunday in church she paid close attention to the Bible reading, marked the place and on returning home to her room repeated the exercise. She was learning to read directly from the Scriptures without human help. The Old English was no obstacle; she gradually mastered the language. Some months later she returned to her pastor and reminded him of his request for a Sunday-school teacher. Her offer of help was accepted and she was given a class of boys.

For years Mary taught in the Sunday-school and Bible class, watching the boys in her charge come to faith and growing in their knowledge of the Lord. Some of them heard the call of God to overseas service. They were her missionaries for whom she prayed at her ironing board altar.

As we walked back to the village along the snow covered country lane I realised I was in the presence of a saint of God, or was she an angel? Certainly she had ministered to me by prayer, by words of encouragement, and by the warm cup of coffee. She even produced a ten shilling note from her purse and insisted that I should take it to pay my bus fares.

Then as we walked through the flat Essex countryside we passed a few scattered cottages. 'This is my mission field', she said, 'I visit these people regularly delivering our monthly magazine. I don't believe in pushing them through the doors,' she added, 'I always knock and have a chat about the Lord.'

Throughout the many years of my Christian life it has been my privilege to see God at work in answer to prayer and faith. Yet it is often through the devotion and sacrifice of people like this dear old lady that it has been possible. To them I shall be eternally grateful.

On many occasions we have to wait for long before we receive the answers to prayer which we desire. At about this time in my life we were in contact with the Corless family. Mrs Elsie Corless began to attend the ladies meetings that were started in the Malletts' home. She was a devout Christian and brought her two children to Sunday school. Her husband however did not believe although he always treated us courteously when we visited their home. Pray as much as we would, and talk to him about the Lord, but he could not see the way of salvation nor would he attend church.

After many months an amazing thing happened. One Saturday morning he told his wife he was going out alone on his bicycle. This was quite out of character as he was a strong family man and rarely went out alone except to go to work. He was away for several hours but when he came back his wife could see a remarkable change in his demeanour. He could not suppress his joy as he told that he had received Christ into his life that day.

It soon became apparent that unknown to any of us he had met Christians in the factory where he worked near Rainham, Essex. He had many serious conversations with them and attended meetings of the Workers Christian Fellowship. Finally they had held a special annual event that Saturday in a local church and Mr Corless was invited. There for the first time he saw his own spiritual need and understood how much God loved him. He confessed his need, repented of his sins and received the Lord.

We were all so surprised at the change in that man's life and how God had taken matters out of our hands but had answered our prayers. He truly was a new man; his wife could vouch for that. From then on he became an active member of the church helping in many practical ways and always at the prayer meetings!

Further Education

Esther arrived in March 1955. As when our son David was born so also it was in the case of our daughter, we were very poor. But God wonderfully provided. Everything necessary was there when it was needed even down to the midwives, three of them (all Christians), though only one of them was needed at the delivery!

To help out with expenses I looked for suitable work. The idea of taking up secular employment was distasteful to me not because of what it was but rather that I became increasingly aware of the importance of the work of evangelism and church planting in which I was engaged. The field was white for harvest but the labourers were few. However, even the Apostle Paul returned to his trade of tent making when the need arose so I was willing to do whatever was necessary. Dorothy was able to get some casual work doing relief clinic nursing at the local health centre. Later she was invited to do some district nursing visiting many homes on the estate. This was not only a means of income but also an entrance into families, which would otherwise be closed to our Christian witness. Her work made an important contribution to the evangelistic outreach and church planting in which we were engaged.

From time to time I was invited to take part in religious assemblies in local schools. I did so enjoy that. Often there were children who knew me and I was always made very welcome. In contrast when I was doing door-to-door visitation in the mornings people were often out or too busy to talk. This made me begin to think that I would be much better employed teaching in school, if I could get in. Someone told me that one of the local secondary schools was very short of staff so I applied but I was refused.

Some months passed by and I became even more convinced that I should be teaching in school. Then I saw an advert in a newspaper for a teacher of religious knowledge at the same school that had rejected me. We made it a matter of prayer and I applied again. There is something to be said about persevering, for this time the headmaster asked for me to see him. As I did not possess the formal qualifications he had been reluctant to take me but after seeing me and learning of my experience and the training I had received he took me on.

This was a temporary position. I was offered a salary that was much greater than I had expected as I had applied to be part-time so that I could continue with my other work. The post would be subject to confirmation after the Essex Education Department had received my application forms and looked at the original documents I possessed. I started work immediately in September but it was not until after Christmas when we were still passing through a financial crisis that I heard that my pay had been reviewed. Perhaps the amount so far, I thought, was temporary and now I would receive a cut in pay. In fact when I opened the second letter they had doubled my pay enabling me to pay all my bills.

I now found myself as the only teacher of Religious Education in a school containing 850 pupils. As I was part-time the head teacher re-arranged the school timetable so there were enough lesson periods for me to teach them all. That was fine but extremely busy for me when there were exam papers to mark and report books to complete for each student. That required many all night sittings but I had found what I was looking for, an opportunity to reach the unreached for Christ.

Whenever possible, I set the children homework that required Bible searching. That meant that each family needed to own a Bible and get it out and use it. If there was no Bible in the home I offered to find one for them. I was gratified to know that by this means many families were being awakened to spiritual things. Of course it helped that I lived on the estate whereas most of the staff commuted from a distance. Sometimes when I was visiting from door-to-door the children would identify me as their teacher that led to some interesting conversations with their parents.

The school was overcrowded, it was built for 500 to 600 pupils but at that time we had 850. I taught in every available room, the dining rooms, workshops, the art department and so on. On Thursday afternoons I had a whole third year (200 plus fourteen year olds) to myself. This was an ordeal by fire, they were used to no discipline at this point and used to lever the rubber feet off their chairs and throw them at the teacher! I was not going to put up with it and left the room (the main hall) to consult the headmaster. However, outside the door I made it a matter of prayer and asked the Lord to help me. Also I did not wish to admit defeat to the head. Having prayed I returned, caught one boy in the act of mischief and decided to make an example of him. Everyone calmed down and from then on they seemed to respect my authority which came from a genuine desire to teach them something good administered with firmness and a strong sense of humour.

Disciplining the boys was far easier than dealing with the girls. Even in those days when corporal punishment was allowed the girls were off limits and they knew it. One class of girls was so difficult that with Dorothy's permission I invited them home for tea! What could you do with those who only went out with their mother to do shoplifting? When they found someone who had a sincere interest in their welfare and was prepared to give them time they appreciated it. Of course not all the girls were like that, some came from very good homes.

Shirley came from a good family but she was one of those who got up to innocent mischief and was always chattering when she should not. Frequently at the end of class I would have to call her aside and give her a talking to! On one occasion when she was in my class I noticed she was sitting beside a girl whom I had not met before. The girl whose name was Trish was wearing the badge of Girl Covenanters, a Christian organisation. When I asked which group she belonged to she said that she used to belong to one in Harlow but since moving to this new house she had not found a place to go. I turned to Shirley and enquired if she knew where our church was and when her answer was in the affirmative asked if she would mind making arrangements to bring Trish next Sunday morning. Sure enough they were both there and joined our girls' Bible class.

In the months that followed I do not know what became of Trish but I do know that Shirley became a committed Christian and eventually married Bob Bell to whom I referred earlier. They became active members of their local church. Shirley's brother also became a Christian and married a girl from the Belhus Chapel and set up a Christian home.

How many other worthwhile results there were from that period of teaching in the Lennard School, I do not know. It was certainly a learning time for me and paved the way for what was to come.

We were now living on another London County Council housing estate called Kenningtons. The church at Belhus was well founded and the new chapel was open. We viewed ourselves as missionaries and not pastors and therefore it was time to move and we were able to rent another house from the council in Usk Road.

Our friend Audrey Garrard, a local midwife, had found another Christian family. Sid and Pam Holden, were a fine young Christian couple, who soon threw in their lot with us to begin planting another church.

Once again our home was used for youth meetings and Bible Classes. We were also able to hire a local school hall for Sunday school. There were many children on the new estate and we were the only people doing this kind of thing for them.

Soon we were joined by Jim Bass a keen Christian living in the nearby village of Aveley. He brought his two boys, Alan and Colin, and they became part of the fellowship. Jim became the church secretary and Sid Holden the church treasurer. Many years later both Alan and Colin Bass became overseas missionaries.

For three years we worked on the Kenningtons estate but saw little fruit for our labours. Throughout that time we got to know Mr and Mrs W W Vellacott much better. He was a local farmer whose family had farmed in the area for generations. William had put much time and effort into the Belhus Chapel in the later years of its founding and was a trustee. I declined to be a trustee or even a founding member because at that time I still felt a real call to India and did not expect to be in Essex for long.

In the nearby village of Aveley were several believers who were concerned about the lack of evangelical witness in the area. After prayer we decided that as we were not committed on Sunday evenings we could start some services in the local village hall. These we held for several weeks and more people began to attend. It soon became clear that many of these were Pentecostals and as we were not we felt that we should face up to the issues then rather than have difficulties later. A special meeting was called and we gently stated what our position was and that they would be allowed the choice, either I would remain the leader but it would not become a Pentecostal church or if they wanted a Pentecostal church I could not remain as leader. Moreover I said that I was quite willing to remain until they found a Pentecostal pastor. The discussion was quite amicable and the decision was made, I continued to lead for a few months until they found someone and then I stood down. Some years later I was in the area and noticed a new building that became the home for the Aveley Pentecostal Church that began its days as I have described in the village hall.

A Man Called Bugby

Paulerspury is a small village just off the A5 Watling Street in Northamptonshire. It is within easy reach of the villages of Olney and Elstow, and the small town called Lutterworth. These little known places in the heart of England were cradles for visionaries whose deeds have left their imprint on the whole Christian church and the world at large.

Before printing was invented John Wycliff, the Reformation's Morning Star, made Lutterworth his home where he made the first translation of the Bible into English and from which his Lollard preachers evangelised the land.

The Moot Hall still stands beside the village green at Elstow, where John Bunyan's preaching led to his imprisonment. *The Pilgrim's Progress* was but one of many books which he wrote in jail. They have been translated into many languages and influenced the thinking of millions.

William Carey was born and brought up in Paulerspury. The humble cobbler and village schoolteacher had a vision of a world in need and became the founder of our modern missionary era. Leaving rural England Carey sailed with his wife and children to India where amid great hardships he learned the languages of the orient, translating the Bible into thirty-five of them. He made such an impact for good that two hundred years later the world's largest democracy struck two postage stamps in his honour.

At Olney John Newton, converted slave dealer wrote his famous hymns together with William Cowper. He constantly gave his testimony of 'amazing grace'. At his death he was buried in the churchyard of the obscure village of Olney but not before influencing William Wilberforce the British parliamentarian to bring an end to slavery.

All these, and no doubt many other stories from the Northamptonshire area, illustrate the teaching of Scripture that God has chosen the weak and lowly things of this world to fulfil His great purposes. It was from this same area that Thomas Bugby came.

Our first contact with him came when Mr Bugby attended a 'breaking of bread' service which we held in the hired lounge of the old peoples complex on the Belhus estate. He was a small stocky quietly spoken man dressed for riding his two-stroke motor cycle and wearing his customary 'beret' on his head. We soon learned that he was a London City Missionary working among seamen at Tilbury and the London Docks.

It took some time to get to know this modest eminent man of God. We learned that during the First World War he had been conscripted into the British Army and sent out to Palestine in the Middle East. There he began to take an interest in the local people and wanting to communicate he tried learning the Arabic language. He soon became proficient and found that he had a gift for languages. Already he was a keen Christian with a desire to share his faith so it was natural for him to reach out to the Palestinians with the gospel. For this he acquired Bibles and Scripture portions from the British and Foreign Bible Society. He was so successful in this distribution that when it was time for him to be demobilised from the army he asked if he could remain in the country and applied to be the Bible Society's representative in Palestine.

For several years Tom Bugby was an itinerant evangelist in Jerusalem and the surrounding district with occasional visits to Egypt. This meant crossing the Suez Canal, the world's most busy shipping lane. The crews of the great ships that passed through came from many nations. Tom seized the opportunity to send the gospel around the world by distributing the Scriptures in numerous languages. Hindustani was spoken by most of the seamen so Tom set about learning that too. An Indian crewmember once told the writer that Mr Bugby spoke the Hindi better than the natives. From farther east came men from Bengal so the missionary added their language to his list and soon became proficient in that also. Finally there were those from Singapore and Malaysia so he also taught himself to communicate with them.

Visits to Egypt became more frequent when Tom fell in love with the daughter of a missionary of the Egypt General Mission. They married in Cairo cathedral. During the twenties they were based in Jerusalem, but the young Mrs Bugby became ill and her doctor insisted that she would never remain fit if she remained in that climate. To Tom's great disappointment they had to return to England. Tom was a man of prayer and as he brought their situation before the Lord it became clear to him that he could still reach the seamen who passed through the Suez Canal. Of course they were mainly bound for the port of London. Enquiries led him to the London City Mission that had a vacancy for a man at Tilbury. There the Lighthouse mission became their home for more than forty years. It became his base to reach multitudes of seamen who came to the port of London from all around the world. Each week he would receive information regarding the many ships due to arrive at the various docks in the port and he would make plans to meet them.

During the few years in which I knew Tom Bugby I occasionally went with him around the Royal Docks. Sometimes I was allowed to go with him into the crews' quarters of some of the great P&O Liners where he would speak to the men in their own languages. He seemed to know everyone. As they dressed alike in their blue denim overalls these Asian men seemed all the same to me but he told me that he would know if they had taken a new man into the crew!

The doors to the Lighthouse Mission opposite the dock gates at Tilbury were always open when Mr Bugby was at home. Seamen would enter in ones and twos just for a chat around the little stove, or to have their Hindi letters read to them, as many were illiterate. Sometimes they would dictate letters home for him to write. Then there were forms to be filled in. Occasionally he acted as their translator when dealing with authorities or even attending court on their behalf. Always this quiet humble man listened to these men from the east, many Muslim, and gently shared the good news of Jesus with them. Over the years he kept records of more than one hundred thousand who visited his centre at Tilbury. Mainly it was personal work though sometimes he would gather a small company to see slides or a film. Always there was tea available and a cheerful welcome.

There were many seamen who returned each time their ship was in port and some became interested in the gospel and became believers. It was hard for such as their lives were in jeopardy if they made an open stand for Christ. There were occasions when Tom enquired about such a person and was told that he had fallen overboard or met with an accident. He knew it was no accident.

The time came when we felt that the Lord was leading us back to Birmingham and we shared this with Tom Bugby. He urged us to begin an outreach to the men who regularly jumped ship and went to live in Birmingham. Start a City Mission there he urged. He followed this up by giving me the name and address of a Baptist Minister in Bordesley Green who was secretary of the Fellowship of Faith for the Moslems (FFM). Tom was sure that he would help. Then Tom used my newly acquired tape recorder to record messages in Hindi, Bengali and Arabic to play to people from the east now living in Birmingham. In the past Tom had suggested that I joined the London City Mission but I had no liberty in my spirit. Now I felt the challenge and promised that I would do what I could. Thus this man from 'Carey country' played a part in founding the present Birmingham City Mission.

The Kingshurst Story

An old Victorian house in the village of Marston Green stood empty with a large 'for sale' notice by the front gate. Dorothy and I on borrowed bikes pulled up outside considering the possibilities. A District Nurse was leaving the next door neighbour and understanding our enquiring looks said, 'That house is now sold, why don't you try Kingshurst? There are houses for sale there.'

This was not the first time our attention had been drawn to Kingshurst. A few Christian friends were meeting in Aylesford Hall in Shard End. I had expressed an interest in the spiritual needs of East Birmingham, especially in the vast growth of new housing estates in the post-war era. They mentioned Kingshurst to me and Stanley Marshall, my friend who had moved into the area, took me for a drive around the estate that was being built.

Kingshurst Hall was a medieval moated manor house surrounded by woodland near Coleshill, Warwickshire. The land was bought by Birmingham City Council on which to build inexpensive houses for poorer people of the rapidly growing population in the post-war period. The historic hall was demolished and replaced with tower blocks and houses to accommodate about twelve thousand people. We knew nothing of the later development until 1970 when work began on the adjoining farmland and the building of homes to house seventy thousand more people at Chelmsley Wood.

Back in Essex we began to pray earnestly about a move to Kingshurst. The three-year lease on our house in Usk Road was coming to an end and we had no liberty to apply for an extension. The more we prayed the greater the conviction became that it was time to leave Essex and move to Birmingham. As an act of faith I gave in my notice to leave Lennard School where I did part-time teaching. For housing we thought that we would apply to rent a City of Birmingham council house, one of those being built at Kingshurst. As we heard that the estate was outside the city boundary and in the rural district of Meriden and that they also had houses at Kingshurst we applied to rent one from them as well. Our friend Eric Beresford, living in Yardley, Birmingham, made the application. We waited. A letter arrived telling us that we did not qualify for a City of Birmingham council house. We continued to wait until one morning I decided to phone Eric to see if he had heard from Meriden Rural District council. He had heard that day and they also had refused.

The house where we lived in Usk Road had no telephone. On the edge of woodland opposite was a red phone box that we used. Returning from my disappointing call to Eric I was surprised to see our friend and prayer partner, Mrs Emblen, standing on the doorstep. We had not been in touch for several months but she told us that as she had being praying for us the Lord had laid it on her heart to travel from Romford using two buses for the ten mile journey to visit us. 'I understand that you are planning to move to Birmingham', she said, 'Have you got a house to go to?'

I told her about the telephone call I had just made. Then

she gave us an astounding reason for her visit.

'My parents used to own property in Deal, Kent, and after they died it was rented out. The government has made a compulsory purchase order for the building so that they might construct a new road. The money has now come to me and as I prayed about how it should be used the Lord told me to offer it to you to buy a house in Birmingham.' She knew nothing of our applications for housing. The timing of her visit was incredible. As we were not on the phone she could not talk to us beforehand, she just came.

We decided that Ma Emblen's money would be treated as a low interest mortgage towards buying a house at Kingshurst. An uncle of mine had died some months earlier and he also left us a small legacy that we also put towards a new house.

It was now July 1961. Dorothy was expecting our fourth child to arrive in October. As had been our practice for several years we made plans to lead youth camps at Malvern in Worcestershire. We would take over thirty young people from Essex to be joined by others from around the country. They would be with us for one week but we would stay for a month receiving new batches of campers each week. Somehow we felt that we would not be returning to our house in Essex. In fact Dorothy and the children never did return.

All our household goods were carefully packed in boxes and tea chests. Furniture was dismantled and the house was thoroughly cleaned ready for a removal. A packing case full of clothing and items needed for the family during the month at Malvern was sent on ahead by rail. It really was a bit of an Abraham experience. We were leaving home not knowing where we were going. Our trust was in God.

The camp went very well. We had pitched tents in the fields next to the former 'Old Elm' Gospel Hall which was now the permanent centre for the 'Andrew League'. The centre served as kitchen, dining room, meeting room, washing and toilet facilities. We had a small shed in the yard to house our family. The campers arrived on Saturday. On Sunday after service we went up the hillside to Malvern Wells where we played games on the common. Mondays were the days when we climbed the Worcestershire Beacon, the highest of the Malvern Hills. How we enjoyed those days in the beauty of what we called 'Elgar country'. It was hard work looking after so many young people, many of whom had never before had a country holiday. Some had not even seen sheep before. But a lasting impression was made on their lives and for many it was the beginning of their Christian pilgrimage.

In the midst of all this hectic activity we felt that we should take a day off and explore the possibility of buying a house at Kingshurst. Malvern is thirty-seven miles from Birmingham. We spent several hours searching for a house for sale in the district. Only one had a 'for sale' notice on it and when we approached the estate agent we were told that it had already been sold.

Disappointed with our visit we went into the city and decided to place an advertisement in the local *Birmingham Evening Mail*. It simply said that we wanted to buy a house at Kingshurst and we asked for replies to be made to my brother John who now lived there. His phone number was included. I made it my prayer that the first reply would be for the house the Lord had for us.

For some days we waited but there was no word from John that anyone had responded to the advert. Then Lily Moulden whose children were camping with us came on a visit. She also lived at Kingshurst and knew my brother. I asked her if she had seen him lately and if he had any news for me. She said that a man from a house nearby had responded but he owned a large house that was too expensive for us so he had not passed on the information. On hearing this I decided to immediately go to Birmingham and see the house for myself.

John had been right, it was a big house and it was worth more money than we could afford. Mr Copsey, the owner, showed me around. It was beautiful and just where we needed to be. There was a long drive and a garage, but we had no car and could not imagine ever possessing one. The garden was well laid out and in full bloom. While there he showed me a pile of letters which he had received from people who wanted to buy his house. It looked as if we were not even in the competition and unlikely to buy it. However our camp was coming to an end and I told him that I would be visiting my brother a week later. If he was interested in my enquiry he could contact me there. As far as I could see he was not a practising Christian but I told him that the reason for us wanting to come to Kingshurst was that we wished to plant a church on the new housing estate.

A week later I visited my brother again and while we were talking in his home the doorbell rang and there was Mr Copsey. 'Would you mind coming round to my house again?' he asked. We went and once inside he confided, 'I don't know why but since you came to my home I have not been able to sleep at night! I keep thinking about you and feel sure that you should have this house. Will you please buy it from me?' When I said I could not afford such a high price he brought the figure down but even then it seemed beyond me. To my astonishment he replied, 'Do you have five pounds?' I think that was all I did have so he said, 'Give it to me. It will pay for the fire insurance and we will make it a deal. I can find the deficit between the money which you have for the house and the lower asking price.' God had provided us with a home in just the right place in a way which made it clear to us that we were moving in His will.

On the day when we had searched in vain for a house to buy in Kingshurst and went into Birmingham City centre to place an advert in the newspaper we also visited the Education Office in Margaret Street. I intended to apply for a teaching post in the city, mainly to help with expenses. It was August and the office was closed and the building was being renovated. We returned to Malvern empty-handed.

However after making the decision to purchase Mr Copsey's house we felt confident that the Lord would provide. Of course there were all the legal formalities to go through before we could move in. It was decided that I should return to Essex in preparation but Dorothy and the children should remain in Birmingham, she and the youngest with her mother and the other children with relatives.

It was a lonely and strange experience for me to live in the house in Usk Road with all our belongings packed ready to move. But it was not far from the solicitor who was dealing with the legal transfer of property and I was on hand to sign documents.

I was still convinced of the value of teaching Scripture in schools and I also needed to find means of income. The *Times Educational Supplement* usually contained a list of teaching job vacancies from around the country. Having bought a copy from W H Smith in Upminster I sat on a park bench and looked for the Birmingham Advert. There was none. Usually there were scores of vacancies in that city. Clearly their renovations had led to them failing to advertise that week. It was very frustrating for me. Then I remembered that Kingshurst was in Warwickshire just outside the Birmingham boundary. I looked for vacancies in the county of Warwickshire. There was one for a teacher of Religious Knowledge at a place called Kingsbury (not Kingshurst). I looked on the map and found that it was about eight miles from Kingshurst. It would have to do, so I immediately wrote to the County Education Office in Warwick. The reply that soon came was surprising. They said that they were sorry but the job had been taken. However they enclosed blank application forms and suggested that I returned them filled in but not naming a school to which I was applying. I have never heard of such another instance as this.

A week or so later I received a letter from the Headmaster of Kingshurst High School for Boys asking me to go and see him. Dorothy's brother Fred Perkins, a missionary in Algeria, was on furlough at the time and he took us to the school in his car that September evening. They waited outside in his car while I went in for the interview.

Mr Fred Aldridge was a strongly built dark-haired formidable middle-aged man whose manner was at times abrupt and overbearing. He was one of those who cared not for man or God and was not afraid to say so. We met first in the woodwork shop where he spent a lot of his leisure time. He took me into his office, looked me up and down and then began to read my application forms. 'I don't know why they have sent you to me,' he observed, 'I've already got a Religious Education Teacher and we are the best staffed school in the county.' His attitude to me was decidedly discouraging. He continued to read, then abruptly said, 'You seem to have had a sudden change in your life!' I took this to be my cue. It looked as if I would not get a job there but at least I would share my testimony to what God had done for me so I did just that. When I told him of the open-air meeting where I first heard the Good News he asked me where it was. I was of course applying from Essex. When I told him that it was in Yardley, Birmingham, he asked which church the preachers came from. 'The Gospel Hall, in Waterloo Road, South Yardley,' I replied. The man sat back in his seat and went quite pale. It was almost as if someone had hit him. His tone of voice changed completely. 'Does not my name mean anything to you?' he whispered. In a flash I could see that he was the son of the man who baptised me and had been one of the preachers in the open-air meeting. Fred Aldridge had been brought up in that church but through pride and unbelief had turned from God. I was amazed. After a long pause he added, 'I think I had better find you a job. What else can you do?' There were a number of boys in the school who needed one-to-one teaching. Although they were over twelve years old there were those who could not read. He asked if I would help. I insisted that if I did some Bible teaching I was willing to help out anywhere I could.

I began teaching at Kingshurst High School for Boys in Cooks Lane on 1st October 1961. That week I taught Scripture to two classes of boys. I asked if any of them belonged to a youth organisation. No one did. I then invited them to attend a meeting of a new group. We had already met David and Phylis Torpey whom were keen Christians living nearby and, as we still hadn't finished the formalities for buying our house I asked if this meeting for boys could be held at their house. Twenty-four boys attended that first Covenanter group. The Covenanter Union was a Christian youth organisation which both David and I had experience with. One boy at that first meeting and from the first class which I taught was Ray Wootton who has continued in the faith for over forty years and serves as an elder and youth leader in the church. Hundreds have come and gone since and many have continued in the Christian life, some as missionaries, pastors and leaders elsewhere and in many countries.

The formalities for buying the house being concluded I had to arrange for a removal van to transport our furniture from Essex to Kingshurst. I was completely out of money and prayed earnestly that God would provide. As the men were loading up the van, the postman arrived. There was a letter from someone enclosing a gift of money, the only time that person ever sent me any. It was just the right amount to pay for the removal. We moved into the house and trusted God to supply our needs. They were met but always with little to spare. Our fourth baby was almost due. We went shopping for a pram and saw just the one we wanted. It was Saturday and the shopkeeper asked when the baby was due. We said, 'Tomorrow!' and the next day Dorothy went into labour. Martyn John was born on 22nd October.

The first week in which we were in the house we called the few local believers, my brother John and his wife Jean, David and Phyllis Torpey, Lily Moulden and John and Muriel Wager together for prayer. We began to pray that God would send us other members. We had noticed that in Gilson Way, no more than two hundred yards from our house a new block of maisonettes was being built. We prayed earnestly that a Christian family would move into the block. By the time our next meeting was held Dorothy was in hospital with the new baby. I went to visit her leaving instructions that the prayer meeting should continue without us. By the time I returned the meeting was in progress. I knelt down and prayed, mentioning once again the need for a Christian family in the new block. I was touched on the shoulder and someone whispered to me that our prayers had been answered. A slip of paper was pressed into my hand having on it the name Sidney and Hilda Saunders and the address of the block in Gilson Way. That couple became faithful members of the new church and though they moved away continued to support our work in the Birmingham City Mission and Hilda and daughter Doreen are members of Kingshurst Evangelical Church at this time.

Children soon make friends with other children and ours were not an exception. Within a day or two they were playing with the boy next door and other local boys and girls. On Sundays it had been our practice to take our children to Sunday school but as we did not have one we suggested that we would tell them a Bible story and sing a few songs in the afternoon. 'Why don't you ask your friends to come as well?' we asked, 'But be sure they ask their parents first.' was the beginning. Within a few weeks the room was full of children on Sunday afternoons. We needed to find larger premises.

The only public building available was Overgreen Hall built by the City Council for the benefit of tenants on the estate. Unfortunately we found that a group of Methodists had booked the hall on Sundays. On enquiry we found that the afternoons were free so within a few weeks of our arrival at Kingshurst we were running a Sunday school there for more than fifty children. Later that number grew so it was necessary to move to Yorkswood School where it grew to such proportions that we started another Sunday school on the new Chelmsley Wood estate. Sunday evening services were also begun in the school, first monthly and then weekly where they continued until we had a building of our own.

The boys who attended the first Covenanter meeting came regularly to our house after we had moved in. They came at ten o'clock in the morning, followed by a time of worship for local members, then Sunday school in the afternoon. It was a busy household with our own four children, including a young baby! But we were keen to start the new church and by Easter 1962 we had planned evangelism visiting homes in the district and showing films in Overgreen Hall.

One lady who came as a result of that visitation was Blanche Judd, a young widow who brought her young daughter Maureen. Blanche became a loyal member of the fellowship and was with us until she died in 1997. Maureen married Derek Purnell, one of our Covenanters and former pupils at Kingshurst Boys High School. These were the first of many of our young people to find their partners within the new community that we now called Kingshurst Evangelical Church.

John and Muriel Wager and family joined us in those early days. Their daughter Pauline became an active Girl Covenanter and was the first of our young people to be baptised. Later Pauline became a missionary to Africa with Worldwide Evangelisation Crusade (WEC).

Dorothy and my sister-in-law, Jean, formed the Girl Covenanter group at Kingshurst. Boys were coming to our home as a result of my contact with them at school but we had no girls. We made it a matter of prayer then compiled letters of invitation and distributed them at the gates of Kingshurst High School for Girls next door to where I taught. The group was soon meeting regularly at my brother John's home in Mullensgrove Road. But we felt the need for a Christian on the staff of the girls' school and directed our prayers there. A few months later a new teacher noticed one of our girls wearing her Covenanter badge and said that she used to be in that organisation. This led to us giving an invitation to the teacher, Pauline Lineham from Rugby, to join us. She became a strong supporter and a great influence for good among the girls.

One pupil called Linda spoke to Pauline about her sister who she said was always reading the Bible and asking questions about spiritual things. It became clear that Mormons had visited their home and the sister, Erika James, was interested but not convinced that it was the right way. Pauline was invited to their house for tea and was able to lead Erika to Christ. She also joined our new fellowship. Later she went to Swansea Bible College and then with WEC as a missionary to Chad where she spent many years supported by Kingshurst Evangelical Church.

This was a period of growth when many young people were having life changing experiences and being prepared for their future careers. We were pleased at this time to be joined by a young Welsh teacher who was quite clearly led by the Lord to live at Kingshurst very near to us. He was born of missionary parents who had laboured in China. Howel and Ann Jones brought a good spiritual influence upon our young people.

Within a few months of my taking up the post of Religious Education teacher at the boys school the man who had previously held the post stood down leaving me to be solely responsible for the religious teaching of more than four hundred boys.

At a parents day Wesley Erpen's mother and father came to see me. They were concerned that their fourteen-year-old son had told them he was interested in becoming a missionary. I encouraged them by saying that he had a long way to go but he could do a lot worse than that. God only knew then just how far he would go.

Two other parents who expressed their interest in the way their son was responding to Christian education were Mr and Mrs Nicholds. They were quite positive saying that they did not know what I was teaching the boys but whatever it was it was good. Their son Owen's behaviour had become all that his parents could wish. He was an early riser and usually brought them a cup of tea first thing in the morning! Owen Nicholds has gone on to be an elder and the church secretary, of Kingshurst Evangelical Church and a director of Birmingham City Mission.

Our family was also growing up and was very much a part of this new church. Financially we were still quite poor. In order to do the work I cut down the number of hours I taught in school and therefore was paid less. Dorothy was now working first as a nurse caring for premature babies at Marston Green then as a Health Visitor at Erdington and Castle Vale. It was still necessary for us to trust the Lord for His provision.

This was also the period when one Monday evening in October 1965 at our Boy Covenanter games evening at

Yorkswood School some of the lads rushed to me shouting, 'Sir, there's some men here to see you!' It was the beginning of Birmingham City Mission. It is at this point that my book, *Into The City*, begins. The book covers a period of twenty-five years starting with this occasion when friends who had been attending an event in the city had chatted about the spiritual needs of Birmingham. One who knew me well was John Powers and he had heard of my interest and burden for a city mission. He had brought them to see me. I took them home to Wheeley Moor Road and shared my thoughts with them.

On Monday 29th November 1965 we gathered other interested friends to a meeting in our home at Kingshurst. There it was decided to begin a 'Birmingham City Mission'. The meeting was minuted and copies were distributed and I still have mine. From then until we obtained rooms at the rear of 36 Bromsgrove Street in 1968, 46 Wheeley Moor Road became the office and postal address for BCM besides continuing to be used for the church. This put a great deal of pressure on our family but we were constantly dependent upon the Lord and lived in a world of miracles.

Teenage children have their own special needs. On one occasion our son David was concerned about the state of our piano. It had originally belonged to Dorothy's mother. We used it regularly for meetings in our house. David had learned to play it. He was being taught by one of my colleagues at school and was doing well. However his teacher had said that now he was studying for his grade five examination David really needed a better piano. I could not see how we could possibly buy one. Money was short and there were plenty of other priorities.

David grumbled. He had gained entrance to the prestigious King Edward School in Edgbaston and was doing well. At home he was learning to play the piano but he constantly asked for a better instrument. At length I said, 'Look David,

I know it is important to you and I would like you to have one but we simply can't afford it. However you know what we do when we are in situations like this; we pray.'

We got the family together beside the piano and prayed that the Lord would meet the need. Then we got on with our normal business as a family does in an early evening in winter. About half an hour later the telephone rang. It was our friend Peter Jackson, the blind pianist. As I recall this was the only time Peter ever rang me. 'Edwin,' he said, 'Could you do with a piano? A friend of mine is going abroad as a missionary. He has disposed of all his furniture except for a piano. He asked me if I knew anyone who might give it a good home, and I thought of you!'

It is true that Peter knew our piano because he used to tune it but I had not seen him for a long while. The timing of his call was providential. The owner would be content to receive a donation towards his travelling expenses. At that time I had thirty pounds. For that money David had an excellent piano which is in the family's possession to this day.

The Sunday school, which had started in our house, had continued to grow, first to Overgreen Hall, then to Yorkswood School and as the population of the area grew another was started in Woodlands School. The district was crying out for someone to visit on the lines we did in Essex. We were therefore excited to receive an application at the city mission from a young couple who were just finishing their studies at Birmingham Bible Institute and about to get married and were willing to work with us. My dual role as leader of the Kingshurst Evangelical Church and Birmingham City Mission seemed ideal at this time as we could see the benefit to all parties concerned.

Ian and Barbara Prior were to be married at Whitsun and I had promised that we would find them accommodation in our area. That was easier said than done! I have always believed that in the life of faith there is a partnership, we have to do our part and the Lord will work for us. On this occasion we could only search for affordable available property but all our looking seemed to be in vain. For several weeks we scanned the newspapers and every other means by which lettings would be advertised but nothing appeared. Now it was getting urgent for the couple that was about to be married and after their honeymoon they would arrive.

On the bank holiday Monday I was free to do some gardening at home. As I needed some extra plants I suggested that Martyn, our youngest son, might like to go with me to Coleshill where I could obtain them. On arrival we found the shop closed so we began our journey home. I did not often go to this small historic town even though it is less than two miles from where we live. As we travelled along the High Street I glanced at a shop and noticed some advertising cards in the window. On impulse I stopped the car and we got out to look. To my amazement there was a card stating that there was a flat to let in Coleshill for only five pounds per week, ridiculously cheap even for those days. I made a note of the telephone number and hurried back home from where I made the call and was assured that the place was still available and that the details were correct. Within minutes we were back in Coleshill as the flat was above an Antique Shop in a quiet part of the High Street in which we had seen the advert.

The flat had self-contained rooms at the back of the shop and the whole of the floor above. I was astonished at the smartness of this newly fitted out and freshly decorated apartment. Then I was told the reason. The owner of the Antique Shop had a daughter who was to be married. He had arranged for the flat to be prepared for the newly wed couple for them to live in. Unfortunately things had gone wrong between them and they had called off the wedding at the last moment. Sadly the shop owner decided to let the accommodation to someone else so he decided to place an advertisement. When I asked when he had done this I discovered that the card had been put in the window only half an hour before I had seen it. Once again we were reminded that we were in God's hands and if we seek first his kingdom all that we need will be ours.

From the outset we felt that it would be necessary to have our own church building. Not that we considered a building to be of prime importance, God lives in His people not in temples made with hands. Our priority was to bring others to Christ and then see them added to the church which is his body. Nevertheless a place of our own in which to worship and serve the local community was seen to be desirable. Within a few weeks of our arrival at Kingshurst we therefore made an application to the city council for land on which to build. The reply was negative. All available church sites on the estate were already allocated they said and it was not possible at this time to meet our request. The expression, 'at this time' puzzled us but gave us hope. A few years later news of the development of the surrounding green belt and the plans to build the Chelmsley Wood housing estate. The population would increase by seventy thousand people within four years. Immediately we applied for a plot on which to build a church. Eventually we obtained one in Cooks Lane, where the church now stands, opposite the Kingshurst estate.

Each day when I walked to the school where I taught I passed by fields on which horses grazed. It was on the low ground near the River Cole that we were offered a site for a church. It was not good prospect because of a small stream that passed through the land, and the site appeared as a large hole, which needed to be filled in. However, houses and tower blocks were being built alongside. We would be with the people.

In March 1970 a dedication service was held around the 'hole'. Other Christian friends from around the city joined our local believers. Dr David Rigby, principal of Lebanon Bible College, Berwick-upon-Tweed, was the guest speaker. Dr Rigby had served as a medical missionary in Guyana and India before returning to England to train others. Six students from Kingshurst and several others from Birmingham City Mission went to his college for training. Also a number of former students at LBC came to work at Birmingham City Mission.

The acquisition of the church site was a step of faith. We had no money. As we stood around the plot of ground that Saturday afternoon we reached out in prayer and even as we did so someone pressed an envelope into my hand. Later I found that it contained one hundred pounds, a lot of money at that time. God was encouraging us to move forward.

Within a few weeks we had enough money to pay for the hole to be filled in. Then we had plans drawn up for the new church building. It had been suggested that a Christian architect did this work and meetings were arranged for us to discuss with him our requirements. It soon became clear that he did not share our vision and was very dubious regarding whether we could meet the financial responsibilities. The process was long drawn out but eventually plans were drawn and permissions obtained. A contractor was engaged to lay the foundations, which entailed pile driving many feet to the rock beneath. A platform then had to be constructed across the site before building could be commenced. This cost a lot of money and when this stage was completed we were out of funds.

Months went by and we still could not see how we could afford to pay for a new building. So far we had avoided any debt, but we were still a small community and our young people were not earning. But God was with us and encouraged us.

We were in an area that was entirely new. There were no local established Christian families who could be our benefactors. We were also in East Birmingham which for historical reasons put us at a disadvantage. The First World War had a devastating effect on the district. So many men had died. Soldiers returning from the battlefields were getting married and setting up homes for the first time. New housing estates were built in the Birmingham suburbs, especially on the eastern side in South Yardley, Kitts Green, Glebe Farm, Alum Rock and Ward End. But there was shortage of money and unemployment was high. Few were interested in joining a church let alone taking leadership responsibilities. There were exceptions, the Jefferies brothers held tent meetings in Ward End resulting in a small revival. Many local factory workers were converted and they built for themselves Bethel Temple that opened in 1936. But the Second World War started in 1939. Few other new churches had been opened on the new estates and the generation born between the wars were largely unchurched and untaught in the things of God. At the close of the Second World War the spiritual state of the city was even worse. Many homes had been destroyed in the bombing and when the men came home from the war, got married and had children there was much overcrowding. There was a boom in building new houses in the 1950s and 60s. All around the outskirts of the city new estates were developed including on the east Shard End which served as a national model, Castle Vale, Kingshurst and later Chelmsley Wood.

Daily we were challenged by the unfinished task. The foundations of the new church had been laid and a sign had been erected proclaiming the Kingshurst Evangelical Church would be built on that site. To make matters worse someone wrote to complain that rats had been seen on the site. Not that it was our fault, but it underlined the urgency for us to finish the work we had begun. As we prayed about it we felt the Lord telling us to use the foundations. Then the idea came that we should hold a tent mission on the site.

Two large tents were hired, one a marquee capable of holding a hundred people. These were erected on the concrete platform, the area was fenced and the auditorium furnished. For two weeks in the summer we held afternoon meetings for the children and evening services for adults. This afforded an opportunity to visit the neighbourhood and let the residents know what our intentions were, as well as preaching the gospel in various ways.

At that time I received a letter from the Christian Enquiry Bureau telling the name and address of someone who was interested in hearing more of the gospel. It seemed that this person had received literature from us. However before we had time to visit this address we had just finished a tent meeting when I observed a young man and an older lady looking carefully at our notice board. I went across to them and soon discovered he was the one who had asked to be visited. Philip Smith and his mother Mary came to the meetings and committed their lives to Christ. Philip's wife Hazel was already a believer and soon the whole family were active members of the church. Philip became one of the deacons and later he and Hazel went to Bible College in Birkenhead. He went on to be a minister of the United Reformed Church in Bournville and later the Isle of Man.

For several years the development of the church and the Birmingham City Mission continued while I held my post in the boys' school. Because of pressures on my time I went to the headmaster and asked to be part-time working less hours and of course for less money. He responded by saying that he also was a family man and, in spite of being head of the school he found it hard to meet all the expenses of his teenage children. He told me that when my children were that age they would not thank me that they were deprived from doing what other children did. In fact my three sons all had a higher education and gained degrees and my daughter too did well, and none lacked anything. God has been faithful not only in the detail but also on the long haul.

In 1975 my son David married Annette Kretchmer and my daughter Esther married Jeffrey Greaves. The weddings took place at Chelmsley Wood Baptist Church, as our building at Kingshurst had not yet been completed. This was painful to us but it increased our sense of urgency leading to the completion and opening of the new building in April 1976.

The builder was Norman Trickett, a keen Christian who built many churches in the Midlands. My brother, John, did much of the practical work at KEC. Others who joined us as a result of the tent mission became church members and went to it with great enthusiasm. Hard practical teamwork is an important factor in building a strong Christian fellowship.

The financial needs were met by the sacrificial giving of local believers with a little help from other friends and with a loan from Solihull Metropolitan Borough Council. The church duly paid off this loan within seven years. The Council's involvement created an opportunity for the Mayor to be at the opening meeting where he was presented with a copy of *The Living Bible*.

The first couple to be married in the new church was Wesley Erpen and Jackie Brown. These were both former pupils at Kingshurst High School and members of our Covenanter group. Wesley served for a while with Operation Mobilisation in France, Jackie became a trained nurse, and both went to Bible College in Berwick-upon-Tweed. They returned to Birmingham to work with the city mission and pastor a church in Halesowen. At my retirement from Birmingham City Mission Wesley Erpen became its new Executive Director.

Kingshurst Evangelical Church occupied a great deal of my time for more than twenty-five years until 1987 when with the increasing responsibilities of Birmingham City Mission and overseas missions it was felt the time had come for me to step down from the leadership. God had blessed us at Kingshurst, there was a fine team of elders and deacons without which we would never have succeeded. My brother John was church secretary, David Torpey who was also Administrator at BCM was church treasurer and the membership was growing with many of our young people into able leaders. In October the church gave me a marvellous send off with a delicious meal and generous gifts including the airfare for my planned visit to Pakistan.

We little thought that eleven years later the elders of the church would ask me to return to leadership. Nor did we think that we would have another period of ministry and the blessing of God with the building of a new Community Care Centre with its impact on the local community and the growth of the church.

Arrival in the City

It is unnecessary for me recount the events which are already recorded in the book, *Into the City* but those who read it will realise that God has been at work in the city of Birmingham in our time. Without the Mission the city would be much the poorer, indeed many homeless and destitute people owe their very lives to it's labour of love. How many more would not have heard the good news of Jesus and found him to be their Saviour we shall never know in this life. *Into the City* was published in 1991 and obviously much has taken place since then. It was finished in time for the 25th Silver Jubilee celebrations of BCM.

When Bill Wooley wrote to me from America I had no idea who he was or how he came to have my address. He said he had been reading an article by me and could he be placed on my mailing list. I did not know then that he was the Executive Director of the International Union of Gospel Missions. Later he wrote inviting me to one of their Conventions. At last in 1987 Dorothy and I attended the 74th IUGM Convention in Syracuse, New York.

We stood on a dark damp evening outside the university Sports Dome where the final meeting had been held. Joni

Eareckson Tada and her husband gave the address. Joni, the famous paraplegic author, inspired us and two thousand people, including several hundred in wheelchairs, invited to the closing banquet. Now we were waiting for our bus to take us to our accommodation. A tall man who could easily be mistaken for film star John Wayne stood beside me in the queue. He soon recognised my British accent and commented that he had heard that we were there and introduced himself as Stephen Burger, the President of IUGM. As we parted I said with tongue in cheek that we could do with a conference like this in Birmingham, England.

Perhaps it was because of my trip to USA that the next year I received an invitation to a conference of city missions hosted by Sydney City Mission in Australia. Somehow, although the expense was great, I felt it my duty to accept and in October 1988 I was the only European to attend. There I made friends with Bruce Duncan, Director of Cape Town City Mission, South Africa and others from the Philippines and Hong Kong. After the conference I visited City Missions in Adelaide, Launceston, Hobart and Melbourne, learning so much of the value and influence of such work.

There was a banquet in Sydney to mark the closure of the conference and I was invited to ask the blessing. I had been seated between two members of parliament of different political parties in order to keep the peace and also to witness to them! Stephen Burger, who was chairman of the banquet, introduced me and in doing so said that the next City Missions Conference would be in Birmingham, England, the first time I had heard of it since my remark in Syracuse.

Soon after my return to Birmingham I began to pray and think of the possibilities. 1991 would be the 25th anniversary of Birmingham City Mission. It would also be the year of the opening by the Queen of the grand new International Convention Centre in the city. I therefore wrote to their office and asked about the possibilities of holding a world city missions conference in the new building. Immediately I received a favourable response, a representative arranged to come and meet me in my office that was then above our bookshop in Bristol Street. She was enthusiastic and offered to provide literature and even someone to accompany me to America to discuss the project with IUGM. In the event that was not necessary but clearly things were on the move. This time I wrote to Stephen Burger and received an invitation to present the project to his board at their next Convention to be held in Winnipeg, Canada. They kindly financed this visit and I was able to convince them of the feasibility of holding a world conference in Birmingham. To confirm that it was agreed that a delegation from USA and Australia should visit the International Convention Centre, which was still in course of construction.

Never shall I forget that tour of the magnificent Symphony Hall nearing completion, and the huge prestigious Hall One where each seat had its own language console and where the stage was large enough to drive and turn around a double-decker bus. We were shown the purpose built conference rooms and the spacious banqueting hall. Stephen and Delores Burger, Charles Chambers from Sydney City Mission and several others had to wear yellow hard hats and were transported by a beautiful new barge along the canal to the landing stage of the ICC. We were all duly impressed, but now the real work would begin to convene a first truly international World Urban Missions Convention.

Space does not permit me to go into details of how we gathered a working committee to oversee arrangements for accommodation, transport, catering and finance. We became very conscious of the hand of God upon this project.

Firstly, the timing was so right. In May 1989 I had attended a European Association of Urban Missions Conference in

Dresden in the then DDR republic in East Germany. Following that I visited East Berlin and viewed The Wall from the communist side. My contacts with European City Missions go back to 1977 when we were guests of the Berlin City Mission. The European Association met every three years and I subsequently joined them in Helsinki and Gothenburg. The conferences were mainly dominated by German City Missions whose purpose was to support missions in Communist countries. An international conference allowed dialogue across the boundaries symbolised by the Berlin Wall. By November 1989 the wall had come down creating amazing opportunities for bringing Eastern and Western mission workers together. In 1990 I actually sat on the now broken Berlin Wall!

Until that time the work of city missions in Europe was virtually unknown by the American missions and vice versa. My visit to Syracuse in 1987 seems to have been a vital link in bringing them together for the common good. A world conference in Birmingham England would be an appropriate catalyst for such a purpose.

Secondly, 1991 would be the twenty fifth anniversary of Birmingham City Mission and it seemed right to celebrate the Silver Jubilee with an event which would glorify God, encourage faith and the spread of the gospel. From the humble beginnings of a few praying believers in local homes, the first open-air meetings in the Bull Ring, and the poor premises in Bromsgrove Street in the early sixties, we have seen God work in wonderful ways. Now it would be the time to tell the story. This became the reason for publishing *Into the City*, as part of the celebrations.

Thirdly, as we approached the authorities for the use of the new International Convention Centre we became aware of their real enthusiasm for a world Christian conference to be held there. Having examined the feasibility from many angles the decision was made, let us go ahead and under

God make it a resounding success.

As I considered the implications of that decision alone in my office I felt very inadequate. At such times I cry out to God in prayer. Then it occurred to me that I might find help in a Directory on my bookshelf. I rang several numbers before being invited to an unlikely address to discuss the project. It was the Opposite Lock Nightclub in the city centre. Had I made a mistake? Standing in the ornate imposing entrance hall I felt I had entered an environment that was completely foreign to me. But then I met the jovial middle aged proprietor who with his broad grin and infectious laugh told me the story of his conversion to Christ. God had turned his life around from the jet setting high life of pleasure to one that still using his organisational skills and many celebratory contacts wanted to serve the Lord. Martin Hone had organised the renowned Formula Road Race through the streets of Birmingham and many other prestigious events. He greeted the challenge of BCM Silver Jubilee celebrations with enthusiasm and prayer.

It was Martin Hone who suggested a parade of flags carried by Birmingham City Mission children as part of the programme. He also obtained Eureka Jazz Band led by Terry McGrath that played 'When the saints go marching in' as flags from the nations represented were carried across the stage. On the night Martin compered the programme in his own inimitable way welcoming overseas visitors with a warm Birmingham humour. Few would have known that he suffered with ME and on that very morning he had felt so low that we had special prayer with him on the stage during the rehearsals.

During the early stages of our preparation we wanted the occasion to be musical fitting the large and grand venue and we also wanted to involve the local churches and our supporters. We therefore invited volunteers to join a special choir and that rehearsals would take place after Sunday services in St Augustine's Church, Edgbaston, where BCM chairman, Rev Ray Price, was the minister. Our own Alan Cutler, senior member of BCM staff and later to become Company Secretary, agreed to be the conductor. He had already conducted a very successful Jubilee Concert for us in Matthew Boulton Hall. This was good preparation for this larger event in the ICC. In good British spirit local church people responded eagerly learning pieces from Kendrick's 'Shine, Jesus, Shine' to sequences from Handel's 'Messiah'.

At another venue an orchestra assembled. Various BCM members who could play instruments were joined by friends from the Birmingham School of Music and began to practise under Alan Cutler's baton. David Dewar, a capable musician, who conducted them in a performance of Elgar's 'Pomp and Circumstance March No 4' joined him. The talented Christian soprano, Anne Linstrum, was invited to sing sequences from the Messiah and also the wonderful, 'Hear ye, Israel' from Mendelson's 'Elijah'. After her beautiful solo the musical part of the programme concluded with a performance, by choir and orchestra of the Hallelujah Chorus and the congregation joined in singing Malotte's arrangement of the Lord's Prayer.

Co-ordinating an event like this was a daunting prospect. Beside the normal running of the City Mission with its outreach and caring ministries the mission had taken on eleven new members of staff and opened a new charity shop at Castle Vale. Clearly we needed help and we were delighted to have the secondment of Ken Harrison from Sydney City Mission to co-ordinate the overall arrangements. In February 1991 he visited England to evaluate the situation, then he came in September with Trish MacDonald and another lady to prepare publicity and programme material for the conference following the Jubilee Celebration. Ken Harrison was a great help as was Rodney Smith, a local church leader who gave much time and expertise to facilitate communication and became floor manager at the conference centre.

Then began the task of sending out invitations. To our great satisfaction the first citizen, Lord Mayor of Birmingham, Councillor Bill Turner, and his wife the Lady Mayoress, both agreed to take part in the event. Steve Burger arranged for the Board Meeting of IUGM to be held in Birmingham, so ensuring a good attendance from America.

The European Association of Urban Mission (EAUM) had provided me with the mailing list following the Dresden conference and that gave opportunity to invite representatives from across the continent. During the years of the Cold War when travelling to Eastern Europe was severely restricted, Paul Toaspern had been able to visit many Communist countries. He had been a pastor in Western Germany at the time the Berlin Wall was being built and people were fleeing from East to West. He had prayed with his family and decided to move from West to East as he felt God told him he would be needed there. I met him first, having gone through Checkpoint Charlie, in East Berlin, in 1977. He was then Director of East Berlin City Mission. It would take another book to tell the story of this wonderful man of God who suffered much for his faith. He was University Professor in two disciplines and an able linguist, writer and poet. It was a privilege to call him my friend. While Paul was not able to return to the west, even to attend his own mother's funeral, he was permitted to travel east. There he visited city mission work in Hungary, Romania, Bulgaria, East Germany and even the Soviet Union. The addresses that he provided were the ones to whom we wrote our invitations.

Besides these, and, of course, city missions throughout Great Britain, we invited similar works in India to send representatives. I had been visiting Operation Mobilisation teams in India since 1978 and had recently visited a work in Bombay headed by Mrs Jaya Thasiah. It was called the

Bombay Revival & Prayer Band and was an admirable work of city mission in the dreadful slums of Bombay. These also were invited.

Financially, we embarked on a careful budget. For many of the overseas visitors we arranged free accommodation in homes. For those who could afford it we drew up a range of hotels and guesthouses at various prices. The cost of the ICC was the biggest hurdle, but even that was negotiated to an affordable cost. We worked out an overall charge for the world conference, a week of meetings in ICC including Hall One on the Saturday night. This came to an inclusive figure that was included in the registration fee. Tickets for the Silver Jubilee were sold to local people for £5. The money from that more than covered costs and helped to pay fares for some whom had come from poor countries. IUGM sent money in advance to pay deposits and BCM underwrote the shortfall of the whole conference. It was well worth it.

October 1991 was exactly twenty-five years after the inauguration meeting of Birmingham City Mission. From those early days, when a handful of ordinary people met for prayer and then ventured out to tell the good news of Jesus Christ on the streets and the doorsteps, God has done wonderful things in our city. The Silver Jubilee Celebration on October 26 was a testimony of praise to God who is able to do immeasurably more than all we can ask or imagine.

The service was attended by more than one thousand two hundred people. There were one hundred and fifty delegates from around the world. They came from Australia, Brazil, Cameroon, Czechoslovakia, Eire, Estonia, Finland, Germany, Ghana, Hungary, India, Nigeria, Poland, Romania, Scotland, South Africa, Spain, Sweden, USA, USSR and Zambia.

The Lord Mayor delivered an address of welcome to Birmingham. Delegates to the World Urban Missions Convention were introduced by Martin Hone, followed by the parade of flags of the nations.

The rendering of 'Shine, Jesus, Shine'[9] by orchestra, choir and audience was quite new to many and from then it became a favourite of the Americans and was sung from coast to coast. A safety curtain across the whole width of the stage had hidden the choir and musicians from view until the song began. When the curtain was raised there was an audible gasp from the onlookers. The astonishing display of colour and sound was quite spectacular.

Rev Ray Price, BCM Chairman, presented the Annual Report of 1990–1991 and this was followed by an audio-visual presentation of the mission. My book *Into the City* was then launched with interviews by Ken Harrison, Charles Chambers (Sydney City Mission), Rev Stephen Burger (IUGM), and Raimo Sinkkonen, Director, Helsinki City Mission. The main address was given powerfully by Rev Bruce Duncan, Director of Cape Town City Mission.

We have since visited many of the places that were represented on this occasion. Across the world people are still talking about the encouragement and testimony of that event. We praise God for it all. The whole programme was recorded on tape and on video and has been widely used.

The next day was Sunday. Many churches had requested speakers from the conference and that provided opportunities for Christian fellowship across barriers of race, language and culture. Friendships were made which were to last for many years. In the evening all the delegates, their hosts and other well wishers, gathered for a service of dedication at St Martins in the Bull Ring. The church was packed and many of the foreign visitors took part, including Mrs Jaya Thasiah whose small Indian figure dressed in a sari standing at the lectern made an indelible impression on our minds.

The International Convention Centre in Birmingham is one

of the most prestigious in the country. Queen Elizabeth had recently opened it and ours was the first Christian conference to be held there. During the following week we made full use of the seminar and lecture rooms, concluding with a splendid banquet in the hall specially built for that purpose.

Somehow it seemed that it was not right that this wonderful meeting of minds from the cities of the world should end. Mission leaders began talking about more conferences of this kind, others about forming an association that would benefit city missions around the world by sharing knowledge and resources. The possibilities were enormous and the feeling was so great that a special business meeting was called on the last day of the conference. Our time at ICC was over so we arranged to meet at the nearby Birmingham Christian Centre.

The chief protagonist was Charles Chambers, head of Sydney City Mission, Australia. He was supported by Stephen Burger, executive director of International Union of Gospel Missions (IUGM) from USA. As I had been instrumental in convening this world conference I was also involved at this early stage. Leaders from several European countries, from Africa, Asia and America, expressed their desire for an ongoing world association of city missions. There were very few objections. Finally, it was democratically decided to appoint a steering committee to lay the foundations of what came to be known as the City Mission World Association (CMWA). On that committee Australia was represented by Charles Chambers, America by Stephen Burger, Africa by Bruce Duncan from Cape Town, Germany by Paul Toaspern from Berlin, Scandinavia by Raimo Sinkkonen from Helsinki. As leader of Birmingham City Mission I represented Great Britain.

The founding of CMWA in Birmingham 1991 created an opportunity for a new outreach to the cities and ultimately an incalculable blessing to untold numbers of poor and needy people around the world. The Lord had ordered our steps and we had arrived in the city.

> If the Lord delights in a man's way, he makes his steps firm; though he stumble, he will not fall, for the Lord upholds him with his hand. (Psalm 37. 23-24 NIV)

Still Following His Steps

Suddenly the noise stopped. From the moment we had taken possession of the old Granville Street hostel we had been subjected to an incredible row. Like most unavoidable irritations you have to come to terms with them and accept them as the status quo. In this case, as well as the all-pervading smell of hops-malt, the problem was Davenport's Brewery that surrounded us. The noise was not only from the manufacturer's machinery, but also from the incessant movement of trucks and heavy traffic, which transported barrels and crates from the depot to retailers throughout the Midlands. It was a constant din day and night.

The mission hostel for homeless men had been acquired from the Church Army in 1979 while it still had sixteen years remaining of its ninety-nine years lease. By the time we had only three more years to run we were becoming anxious regarding the future. I brought the matter to the attention of the hostel management committee on which sat Mrs Delphi Roe, a member of the city council. She put me in touch with the housing department and they organised a search for an alternative building. All was in vain. The only suggestion they made was that they might convert a school for our use in somewhere like Selly Oak, several miles from our present location. This was refused as being unsuitable. Another trawl of council owned properties was undertaken but to no avail, and there was certainly no hope of finding a site within a mile or so of our present central position on which we could erect a purpose built rehabilitation centre for the homeless.

For more than twenty-five years Birmingham City Mission had experienced miraculous answers to prayer. In time of need we had cried to God. We had pleaded his promises in the Bible as a chequebook from the Bank of Heaven, signed by the Lord God omnipotent who is able to do more than we can ask or think. Now we were in another time of need so again we called upon the Lord.

We had explored other options. It had taken months for us to find who was the actual owner of the freehold of our present Granville Street building and by the time it had been established that it belonged to Lady Dudley she had died and the estate was being contested. The heir who inherited it declined to sell us the freehold and asked an exorbitant rent if the lease was renewed.

The hostel staff room, formerly the warden's lounge, stood next to the street right opposite Davenports Lorry Park, the source of most of the noise. At times at the staff prayer meetings we had gazed at the assembled trucks and wished that they would go away and that we could have the site. But the drink industry was prospering and making a lot of money.

Then suddenly the noise stopped. There were no trucks to be seen and a large sign appeared announcing, 'site for sale'. We learned later that in spite of the prosperity of the industry the company was in financial trouble and was closing down the works. God had not deserted us, but it would take another book to describe in detail his provision and the events of the following two years. Of course there was the matter of money, the drawing up of plans, obtaining permissions and the engaging of builders and contractors.

Because if our hostel did not exist the city housing department would have to re-house and continually re-house at great cost many homeless people who could not care for themselves they were very interested in our project. They suggested we went in partnership with Trident Housing Association who was able to apply for government money through the Housing Corporation. The new hostel was to cost about two million pounds that they would fund except for one hundred and eighty thousand pounds that we had to provide for the non-residential area called The Care Centre. Roger P Dudley was appointed architect and we were consulted at every aspect of planning and choice of materials and equipment.

The miracle was complete when the new building known as Washington Court was finished exactly on time. The builders were amazed that everything had gone so smoothly with no accidents or hold-ups. Some said that they had never known such a construction go so well. On 15th July 1995 forty residents of our old Granville Street hostel packed their personal belongings and were escorted just across the street into their new purpose built home.

Councillor Marje Brindle and entertainer Don Maclean conducted the Official Opening of Washington Court on 12th September 1995. Part of the complex was administered directly by Trident Housing. Birmingham City Mission accommodation comprises seven cluster flats with a total of forty-three beds (including five for women, six for people with disabilities and a sick bay) There were actually two opening ceremonies, one for long term BCM supporters and prayer partners which was a meeting for praise and thanksgiving. The other was for officials and staff of the city council, the architects, builders, contractors and many other interested parties. Children from St Thomas's school that had followed the construction as an educational project provided music and singing, a suitable climax for this wonderful event.

The phone rang. Actually in my small office in Acocks Green the phone never seemed to cease ringing but one never knows who may be at the other end. This time someone asked if we could do with another building. Had the caller been able to see down the phone he would not have asked, as there was hardly a square foot to spare. The Arden Road centre contained our general office, finance office, library, youth department, elderlink dining area and kitchen, our main assembly room, toy store, clothing reception and much more.

The caller was a young man who had become a keen committed Christian through some of our young missionaries who had knocked on his door. As he worked in the office of a large construction company he had overheard a discussion regarding their former headquarters that was vacant and being vandalised. The directors were desperate because following an act of arson on the premises the assessors were refusing insurance unless the property was occupied. 'Perhaps a charity would be interested in moving in,' someone suggested, at which our friend interjected, 'I think I know just the charity which would be glad of the offer!'

Again it would take another book to describe all the details of this event, but in the same year that we took possession of Washington Court we moved into our newly acquired headquarters in Watery Lane Middleway, Bordesley. It was provided rent free for two years and then for low rent for some years to come. Within a short space of time the three blocks and two car parks were in use, the central heating had been renewed, windows and ceilings repaired, plumbing put right, floors carpeted and furniture acquired.

The timing was right. We were approached by an elderly

couple responsible for the former railway mission, a few hundred yards from the Watery Lane Centre for help. About the same time Geoff Cable, a former SAS soldier who had a wonderful conversion, applied to be a BCM missionary. We were also buying a newly built house on the Bordesley Village Estate so this was purchased and made available to Geoff and his wife. Soon the whole area was being evangelised.

At the time of writing this chapter (2005) the Watery Lane Centre still serves as BCM headquarters in which I have a small office several years after my retirement. It is forty years since the first meeting of Birmingham City Mission. It is sixty years since that day in 1945 when I heard the gospel being preached outside the public library in Yardley. God laid His hand upon me then, and despite my many failings and weaknesses He has been faithful to me and kept His promises.

Today my wife Dorothy has been to West Bromwich to speak at a women's meeting. She has now gone to her house group at Kingshurst Evangelical Church. The church building has recently been greatly extended, a new care centre has been opened and a new pastor appointed. Again the story of our past eight years since my retirement would fill another book. God is still answering our prayers. He is still on the throne of grace. He has no favourites. He just asks for our trust and obedience and when we fall down He lifts us up and sets us on our way again. Long ago he said to me, 'Follow me, and I will make you to become fishers of men', and 'Seek first the kingdom of God and his righteousness and all these things will be added to you.'

Our family has grown up and all four of our children are married and following the Lord. We now have fourteen grandchildren who are also growing up and are a joy to us.

In the introduction to this book I made it clear that this is not an autobiography but a record of acts of God in the life of an ordinary person in modern times. Were it to be an autobiography it would contain details of family background and childhood. It would also give accounts of my many journeys and ministry abroad, in about thirty countries in each continent. Stories of God at work on these occasions will have to wait. My prayer is that what I have written will encourage others to follow in the steps of the Master.

Notes

1. Edwin R Orton, *Into the City*, Birmingham City Mission, 1991.
2. Mrs Howard Taylor, *The Triumph of John and Betty Stam*, China Inland Mission, 1935.
3. Arthur Mee (ed), *Realms of Gold*, Children's Treasure House (Volume 4), Educational Book Company, 1937.
4. James Moffatt, *The New Testament*, a New Translation, Hodder and Stoughton, 1913.
5. Alfred Bosshardt, *The Restraining Hand*, Hodder and Stoughton, 1936.
6. Johanna-Ruth Dobschiner, *Selected To Live*, Pickering and Inglis, 1969.
7. Alex Rattray Hay, *The New Testament Order for Church and Missionary*, New Testament Missionary Union, 1947.
8. G H Lang, *God at Work on His Own Lines*, 1952.
9. Graham Kendrick, 'Lord the light of your love is shining', Make Way Music, 1987.

Index